Student's Guide
Starting Your Career
AND Earning Money
BEFORE You Get Your Degree

Horace W. Batson, Ph.D.
Gary Batson, D.M.

Foreword by Dr. Leon Perkal
Associate Dean of Faculties (NYSCAS), Touro College

W
WELSTAR PUBLICATIONS

Written with Laura Koplewitz, Ph.D.
Published by Welstar Publications, Inc.
Horace Batson, Ph.D., Publisher
628 Lexington Avenue, Brooklyn, NY 11221.
Phone: (646) 409-0340
Fax: (313) 453-6554
E-mail: publisher@welstarpublications.com
or drbatson@optonline.net
ISBN: 978-0-938503-42-2

Managing Editor: Dr. Laura Koplewitz
Transcription: Carlo Craig
Book Design/Typography, Lori Monroe
Text set in Calibri

Dedication

———————————— ⁓ɰ⁓ ————————————

This book is dedicated to our deceased loved ones - mom, Lila and dad, Herbert and our brother, Ronald Batson (Ron). We still remember mom's never ending encouragement and support.

We can still hear dad's mantra, "Get up early, do your work, go back to sleep and stay in school!" Both Gary and I will never forget Ron's subliminal warning and message that if you press the boundaries of reality and reach for the stars be sure you can come back. Thanks Ron. And a special shout out to Gary's daughter, Phoenix.

Horace Batson, Ph.D.

Gary Batson, D.M.

Table of Contents

———————————— ∿ ————————————

Acknowledgements

—⁂—

Gary and I want thank the countless number of people and events that have help give birth to this book.

We especially want to thank the thousands of students, department chairpersons, professor colleagues, college administrators and support staff whose thoughtful suggestions have helped make this book a more relevant and student friendly reality.

Our heartfelt appreciation to all! Our hats go off to you!

Foreword

It is my honor to commend Dr. Horace Batson and Dr. Gary Batson for writing this groundbreaking and game changing book – "Student's Guide To Starting Your Career And Earning Money Before You Get Your Degree."

Historically, our institutions of higher learning have been charged with the responsibility to teach students the basic elements of their chosen profession, critical thinking and processing skills. To this end we have excelled.

Hardwired into the fabric of education is the (often times mistaken) notion that one cannot earn money in your career until many years of formal education have been completed.

Career books on the market have typically provided students information on how to: select schools and chose a major. They have all stopped far short of teaching students how to actually earn a living in their profession.

Batson and Batson, both professors and entrepreneurs, have challenged our conventional wisdom by positing that students can earn money in their career while and before they actually complete their degree.

Their book guides students, step-by-step, to success. This book is a GPS empowering students to take charge of their lives to harness their hidden potential to jump start their careers and start earning money all while in school.

As you read this book, expand your vision, expand your mind and begin to earn a living in your profession - now!

Leon Perkal, Ph.D.
Associate Dean of Faculties (NYSCAS)
Touro College

Preface

--- ⟋ᵥᵥ⟍ ---

This book is predicated on the belief that all students want to get "A's" for the purpose of eventually earning money in their chosen profession.

Students have been trained to believe that they have to first obtain an advanced degree before they can earn money in their career.

This book challenges this conventional wisdom that it will take years before you get your degree and make money.

Our students' "Guide book" is divided into two parts - Part I-Mindset and Part II- Implementation of The Principles.

Part I is necessary to help students orient their thinking inwards as an introspective workout to enable them to identify their true Life passions (e.g., what you really love to do).

Once you have identified your Life passions and intrinsic skill and interest sets Part II outlines step-by-step, easy-to-follow implementation strategies.

In short, it is our experience that the most difficult part of any journey (i.e., desired destination) is deciding where you want to go.

Once you have discovered your true Life passions and interests (i.e., destination) it will be easier for you to earn money in your career.

The authors want students to understand that you do not have to wait years until you earn a degree before you can earn money in your new career. Your time is Now!

Introduction

---~m~---

*"There is no passion to be found playing small – in settling
for a life that is less than the one you are capable of living."*

~ Nelson Mandela ~

Waking Up to Your Own Life - Every Day!

What do you feel when you wake up in the morning? Do you feel
'Life is sweet' and you look forward to the day, to your job, to
school? Or do you feel, *'I'm dreading this day, I'm bored, I'm not
sure what I'm doing, I'm going nowhere with my life?'* Maybe you
feel some of both.

The question is, what are you doing with the one life you have to
live? Do you love what you are doing? If not, instead of feeling
stuck, there are ways that you can reassess your life direction,
and take steps to change it for the better. That's what this guide
is all about.

Whether you're younger or older, in a new job, or in a job for a long time, starting school, or finishing school, you can choose the next steps in life. You can follow your passions more every day, and find success in doing that. This guide is designed to help you to find out what's best for you.

What do you do with your life, every day? This is an important question. As human beings we have the good fortune of being able to make choices about our lives. This book is designed to help you to make choices. As a guide, this book is not designed to be overly long and complicated. The questions and ideas here are to help you to do the thinking and feeling so that you can discover what drives you most, what your passions are, and how to put a life plan in place that helps you to achieve your highest goals and dreams.

You may ask yourself, as you are looking ahead in life, *'How can I make my life meaningful, interesting, and enriching?'* You may ask, *'What do I care about most in life?'* Often, when starting out or changing schools, starting or changing jobs, moving and joining a new community, beginning a new relationship, you may reflect and ask yourself about the bigger picture. What do you like to do? What are your goals ahead? How can you reach them?

Mark Twain, a famous American author, has said, *"The two most important days in your life are the day you are born and the day you find out why."*

Mark Twain's words are a good reminder that figuring out the "*whys*" in life helps immensely in finding the conviction to move forward with passion, and commitment to becoming the best person you can be. 'Why' helps you to reach for your dreams!

> "*How can I figure out 'why' I have the grace of being alive, here on this Earth? What is my purpose? What road should I choose in my life ahead?*"

Mark Twain says, along with philosophers through time, that finding your path in life is vital! Twain provides us with a question! Who provides the answer? Illustrious sages, authors, poets, spiritual leaders, have all contributed their thoughts towards the answer. You'll find some of their wisdoms here in these pages. But in this little book, *you* are the most important person to both ask, and answer, 'why' and discover 'what'!

Why do you like to spend time on a particular activity in life? Is one life interest a true vocation for you? Should you go to one school or another? Choose one type of job or another? How do you answer these questions - for yourself? Sleepless nights, or worrying a lot, or feeling lost, are often signs that you may want to find answers to the questions 'what' and 'why.' Stumbling upon a direction is one approach. Choosing a direction, however, is the approach that will be longer-lasting. This little book is designed to offer you tools - practical, and spiritual, too-for forging your direction in life, and making fulfilling choices.

"When wisdom comes into your heart and knowledge fills your soul with delight, then prudence will be there to watch over you, and understanding will be your guardian."

~ Proverbs 2:10-15 ~

Choosing a path in life happens more than once! So this guide is for you whether you are just starting out for the first time, perhaps choosing your first college, or applying for your first job. If you've already been in school or working, you may be trying to figure out the next steps that will make your life happier and result in a greater sense of fulfillment on your path.

You may be an individual who feels very settled on your path and in your work, your goals, your relationships. Or, perhaps.... maybe... you are asking questions. "*What if...*" you think... and then immediately after, "*Noooope! Forget that!* " Then again, a few days later, or a week, or a month, you are again thinking, "*Well, really! What if...?*" Again, you stop yourself, "*I couldn't...I'm stuck here.... it's not possible.... I can't make a change...*" And on you go... Life continues... you put changes 'on hold.' *This is just how my life has to be,'* you reason.

"A human heart makes the plans,
God gives the answer."

~ Proverbs, 16-1 ~

When Life Asks You Questions

Every day, when you wake up, you probably have that day's goals in mind. You may have a ' to do' list that you review as you are starting your day. You may be asking yourself: *"Will I get to work on time?"* Or *"Do I need to buy groceries today?"* Perhaps *"Did the dog get walked and fed yet?"* Or *"Is it time for me to do my taxes?"* You may be thinking *"I've got to call my grandmother; she's not feeling well."* Or maybe you're thinking, *"Next weekend is July 4th, what will I do to celebrate with friends and family?"*

Your mind is probably filled with many details about your day, and about the next few days ahead, even the next week, or the next several weeks. You may have a calendar of important *'to do'* tasks. Life can be very filled with the responsibilities we have every day. These responsibilities can take up all of your *'brain power.'* You may feel there's little time in your life to stop for a minute, or an hour, or a day. You just have to keep going, every day.

Most of us live this way. And yet, at times life may be tugging at you with bigger questions. *'Go away!'* you may feel! *'I don't have time to contemplate my life!'* You may simply want the bigger questions - such as questions about your direction in life, your career, your dreams and goals - to quiet down!! Who wants to stop and ask those questions? What if the questions ask for answers that you're not prepared to hear- from yourself! So, everyday life may be filled with many tasks. Perhaps some of these are even designed as distractions. Maybe some of these 'to do' tasks are even enjoyable! Overall, you may be saying, if you're really up front with yourself, '*I'm not ready to re-think my life! It's complicated enough as it is!*'

Your Everyday "To Do" List- What's Missing?

If you make a list of what you think about when you wake up in the morning, chances are, what you are NOT thinking as you start your day is, "*What will make me happy with my life in 5 years?*" You're probably NOT contemplating, "*Do I need to change my career life to match my passions?*"

These issues may be in the back of your mind, indeed, you may even have sleepless nights in which you realize you're not entirely satisfied with your life path. Perhaps it's something that happened on the job. Maybe you are looking at your courses in school, and feeling that you're less than excited about the subjects you're taking. Perhaps it's a larger, bigger picture about life that shows up in your dreams, but not during the daytime.

How good are you at avoiding looking at the bigger picture? Or how good are you at pursuing the bigger picture? Maybe you are in the middle of these questions. For most people, questions that are asked over and over in our minds, and yet remain unanswered, can be a source of constant worrying. You may not even realize that there are questions you are asking yourself. You may hide them away! Instead - nights tossing and turning! An upset stomach! Too many missed days from work! Agitation with friends or family!

> *"Hope deferred makes the heart sick, a prayer*
> *fulfilled is the tree of life."*
> ~ Proverbs 13:12 ~

> *"From too much worrying, comes illusion"*
> ~ Ecclesiastes 5:2 ~

When life ask questions, often it is fear that keeps us from facing the questions. The answers may be much less dreadful than the questions indeed - even comforting!

Let Yourself Ask Questions About Your Life!

What if you were to go right ahead and ask the first question, that leads to *your* answers, for yourself! *"What are my questions about my direction in life right now?"*

What are ways to look at your life more closely, without fear and anxiety! What it would mean if you could make a change, without sleepless nights!

Let's see if we can find pathways into your questions, without disrupting everyday life too much!

Enjoying Your Questions About New Directions

One step at a time is a good way to begin. This book is about befriending your life questions, rather than pushing them away. Instead of bothering you and keeping you up at night, what if you let your life questions begin to be known - to yourself! By *befriending* your questions, and inviting them into your life, instead of being afraid of your questions about your life path - *your questions may become your guides.*

What If I Am Not Good Enough for My Dreams?

"Do not be too severe on yourself, do not let shame lead you to ruin. Do not refrain from speaking when it will do good, and do not hide your wisdom"
~ Ecclesiasticus 4:22-26 ~

What may keep you up at night is perhaps a sense that even though you DO have dreams - big dreams- you may feel you can't step in your own footsteps, fill your own shoes! Thinking about one's big goals in life can have the opposite effect of what we might imagine. Instead of feeling excited, you may find yourself feeling scared. What if you can't 'be' the person you'd like to be? What if you can't follow your dreams, because they are 'bigger' than you feel you are - not in stature, but inside, as a person.

Do you have expectations for yourself? Do you feel others have expectations for you? Do you feel you are living up to your *dreams*?

You may be fulfilling your *responsibilities*, yes. The rent or mortgage is being paid, you've got a roof over your head, you have food, and you are taking care of what's necessary in terms of helping others in your life - friends, family, relatives. But are you feeling fulfilled? You ask yourself, "*Isn't that too much to ask of life? Doesn't that make me 'greedy' if I want to feel more fulfilled?* Do you have a right to wish for this?

Is It Selfish to Dream Big?

The American poet Audre Lorde once wrote in a poem, addressing the reader, and saying, it's OK to have big dreams! She wrote that we all 'hunger' after a better life for ourselves, for our families, and we all have goals and dreams that may yet be unfulfilled. This is part of our humanity, to dream, to imagine, to consider what ' could be,' even as we live our everyday lives. Audre Lorde wrote this: she said, "*... don't confuse hunger with greed... and don't wait until you are dead.*"

The idea that may seem a little daunting, even unsettling, at first, until you think about it. Hunger or greed? Is needing bread and water greedy? Is wanting to choose a better life direction a form of greed, taking away from others? Or could strengthening your life actually help others?

If you think about what your life can be in the future, and what you hope it will be, what do you imagine?

The Plate Exercise: Bread and Honey

Imagine, if you will, that there's a beautiful plate in front of you, and it has bread and honey on it. You have been given that plate and you've been informed that you are allowed to partake, to have this nourishment. Yet as you take the bread, dip it in the honey, and bring it to your lips, you're about to enjoy this wonderful taste, and then - you have doubts. *"Maybe this delicious bread and honey isn't really for me."* Or, *"What if I get into trouble? What if somebody else wants this plate? "* Or *"Do I really deserve this delicious food?* Again you raise the bread and honey to partake of it. Once more, you put it down again. You do not feel entitled. In your confusion, you refuse this delicious nourishment. You decline.

The bread is the basic food of life. The honey is the sweetness of a life fulfilled and happy. This, for many people, is an everyday hunger for fulfillment. For most people in life, the bread and the honey is something they would love to have offered to them. There are those who eat with gusto. Others, more slowly, yet savoring each taste. Others, eat just a little, timidly. Some, not at all.

In Audre Lorde's poem, *"do not confuse hunger with greed,"* she is saying that it's not enough to feel that you're ` *almost'* not hungry, or you are ` *almost'* partaking of nourishment, becoming in life who you want to be.

Others all around you are eating, from their plates. Everyone has been given a plate. It is the nourishment that simply is given to you, for being alive and being human. No one will go hungry if you partake of what you have been given. The bread and honey is the taste of life. Everybody's delicious flavor of life is a little different. On your plate may be your skills, your knowledge, your innate talents. Your bread and honey may be your drive, your curiosity about life. Your food for life may be sitting in the plate you already have.

If are not sure if you should go ahead and be nourished by what has already been given to you - your life, your uniqueness -you, will you have the strength, the energy, for your own life and future? If every day you *almost* partake of your milk and honey, yet reject it for fear of taking too much, how long can you hold out feeling that way? How long do many people, as Audre Lorde says, mistake their own legitimate hunger for fulfillment- for greed?

Tasting Your Talents: Bread and Honey

If you are finding that it is in your nature as a person to ask questions, look at your life, and you wonder what to do with those questions- go ahead and let yourself wonder *"What would that be like, if I dipped in farther, explored my talents, my tastes for interests, skills, passions, and began nourishing my future?* If you take up what is already there, your future, in front of you, and taste it, explore the flavors that are in your life, you will find nourishment. Your life already has the offering of bread and honey. The plate is yours. What you decide to do with it, is your choice, too.

The ancient Chinese poet and philosopher, over 2000 years ago, wrote about nature and humanity:

"By letting each thing act according to its own nature, everything that needs to be done, gets done."

- La Tzu, 6th C. B.C.

If you are already asking questions about making changes in your life, exploring your interests, skills, passions and examining how this will change your life - but then stop yourself short - perhaps you may be ready to go ahead, and let your curiosity get the better of you! Go ahead, explore the food for life that is within you! The nourishment that is yours to take in life, is not a deterrent to others. In fact, your strengths, will help them to find theirs.

Almost may be a word that is positive if you've already chosen a journey, and nourished it, and you are nearing completion of a goal! When you're in school, you may feel you're *'almost'* at the point of graduating. You may feel if you are engaged to be married, that you are *'about to be'* a wife or a husband. These are wonderful anticipations of what *will come.* These are dreams on the way to being fulfilled, and you are *almost* there. How great that you followed your passions and dreams, and you are nearing the achievement of your goals!

On the other hand, the *almost* that comes from not trying, feels very different. It is the *almost* of feeling dejected that you didn't try out your dreams. It's about the *'dream deferred.'*

The African-American poet Langston Hughes, in a famous poem, asked whether a *"dream deferred"* is more like a *"raisin in the sun"* which withers and dries, or does it remain pent-up inside? A dream deferred often does not simply disappear, it can follow you through your lifetime. Why not take courage, face the wonderful opportunity of your dreams, and work to make them come true?

> *"Faith has to do with things that are not seen; and hope with things that are not in hand."*
>
> - *St. Thomas Aquinas*

St. Thomas Aquinas's words remind us that every person born is a unique, miraculous human being. Each of us has been given one life to live, here on Earth. We will live this life, every day, without fail, until we are no longer here on Earth. We know that each life is precious. And so, to treat every day of each as a precious day, is to live with hope *"in things that are not in hand"* as St. Thomas Aquinas has spoken. It is to live with hope and faith in the future.

The Courage to Face Your Future

Having the courage and faith to face *your* own unique future, is a process that can take time. If you go ahead with tools that you can find and learn, the future will not be worrisome. Instead, it will become a pleasure as each *tomorrow* becomes *today*.

A remarkable woman, Helen Keller, who rose beyond enormous obstacles as she was born without either sight or hearing, yet found both light and her own personal calling. As a young woman, Helen Keller was afraid, alone, and felt isolated from the world. Slowly she gained the courage to explore what was around her, and to reach out, literally, to grasp at the unknown, and to lift herself up to feel joy and to make decisions on her own, to become her own person. She said to others who were challenged to take charge of their own lives:

> *"Be of good cheer. Do not think of today's failures, but of the success that may come tomorrow...You will succeed if you persevere; and you will find joy in overcoming obstacles. Remember, no effort that we make to attain something beautiful is ever lost."*
>
> *- Helen Keller*

The time you are alive, the minutes you spend each day, are as precious as hope, and as trustworthy as faith. How do you use the gift of these tens of thousands of minutes that constitute your life? How do you live so that your life is meaningful and worthwhile - for yourself, and for others?

> *"The only limit to our realization of tomorrow will be our doubts of today. Let us move forward with strong and active faith."*
>
> *- President Franklin Delano Roosevelt*

Discovering Your Life's Work

Discovering what is most fulfilling in life, for you, is one way to honor the miracle of being alive. It is a way to fulfill not only your own personal dream, but the miracle of the lives of others, as well. For if you are living to the best of your abilities, then this helps to raise others up to the best that they can be.

What can you imagine for your future, as your personal love of a job you'd like to have? Perhaps it may be that you are instrumental in helping to ease others' pains, as a person who works in health care. Perhaps you are a teacher, helping individuals young and old to learn about the world and discover the capacities of their own ideas! Or you are a skilled worker creating a new design for a building, or helping to develop a new software technology. You may be working in a company as a team member, putting a product out on the market. Or you are working in travel, and facilitating the journeys of people around the globe.

Reaching Your Passionate Goals Helps Others!

Think about what you may be doing today. If you are doing what you love, with passion, and with interest and excitement, do you think it may reflect in your eyes, or your smile, or your ability to be free of worry about yourself, so that you can help other people, and contribute to the world in a positive way? The less you worry about yourself, the more you can help others. Finding your passions in life, and following these passions, frees your energy up! You can share more of yourself in a way that is helpful and loving towards others. Wishing to be fulfilled in your work, in your everyday life, in the use of your skills and talents, is not a selfish activity. It is a goal that, when reached, helps you fulfill the miracle of living, and helps others to fulfill their goals, too.

Another way to think about this question of whether you are allowed to wish for more in your life, is to think about God's hope for fulfillment to come to every human being. No human being is perfect, and we strive each day to fulfill the Commandment to 'Do unto others...'. As the Rev. Martin Luther King, Jr. said, we must summon the courage to speak aloud, to ourselves and others, and say, ' *I have a dream.*' This is the first step towards a journey that may at times feel rocky. Yet, if you start on your path, linking arms both spiritually and actually, with others who are also striving onward and upward, then your journey will not be a lonely one.

You will find friends, mentors, and guides along the way, who are on journeys of their own. In the spirit of empathy and goodwill, they are very likely to open their hearts and minds, sharing what they know and have learned, to help you on your path.

As you find your direction in life, you may discover a truth in the words of Arnold Toynbee, who said,

> *"The supreme accomplishment is to blur the line between work and play."*

After reading this little book and contemplating your life goals, delving into your life dreams, you may find that you can say to yourself and others, with the glow of warmth and sincerity in your eyes:

> *"Today, I arise to lead my life, as a labor of love."*

Student's Guide To
Starting Your Career
AND Earning Money
BEFORE You Get Your Degree

Horace W. Batson, Ph.D.
Gary Batson, D.M.

Foreword by Dr. Leon Perkal
Associate Dean of Faculties (NYSCAS), Touro College

PART I

Mindset

Chapter One

Starting the Journey

Your Life! Your Dreams!

If you are a person who did go ahead seek after a dream or a passion, perhaps you have come to a turning point, too. For, as the sun rises and sets each day, and the world spins on its axis, the seasons change. We grow from youth to adulthood. Our dreams may change as we grow. If you think back to childhood, when you were asked '*What do you want to be when you're older*' you may have jumped right in with the answer!

As a child, you probably spoke aloud about your dreams, without thinking in adult terms, ' *Is this practical*?' Did you know what you wanted to be? Maybe you had a few different ideas! Thinking back, was there a sense inside that you felt you were ' *born' to do,' a* particular thing that you knew you loved?

Did you say, when you were 5 years old, '*I want to be a pilot!*' Or, when you were 10 years old, '*I want to be a policeman!*' Perhaps when you were 15 years old, you said, '*I want to be a teacher!*' or '*I want to own a pet shop!*' Maybe, as a little child, you went with what was right at your doorstep, and said, '*I want to sell ice cream from the ice cream stand!*' Your answer to '*What do you want to be*' may well have been a sudden inspiration! Whether the inspiration was right outside your window, a job that a parent, sibling, or next door neighbor was doing, or a job you read about in a picture book, it began to hold your fascination.

When you look back, was ' pilot,' or 'bread baker,' or 'mechanic,' or 'nurse,' the answer you gave at age 5, and then again at age 12, and then again at age 16? There's a little trend you can spot there! You seem to have been hooked on a particular love!

If you are like many people, your answer may have started out as *pilot* and then changed, instead, to *teacher.* At 5 you said *keep lots of kittens* and at 10 you said, *be a horse jockey.* It's not surprising that our dreams change. Nobody would expect us to commit to a specific ' future' in childhood, and then be forced into staying with that one dream expressed at the age of 5 or 10 or 15.

Maybe it was ' *Raise puppies!*' when you were 5, and then ' *Be a fashion designer!*' when you were 12, and later, ' *Own a toy shop,*' when you were 16. You may have changed the 'type' of job, but there may also be 'likenesses,' in these choices. From a warm, fuzzy kitten, to the soft textures of fabrics, to helping children pick out delightful toys, may have a common theme! You like it when there's a smile on someone's face, and you like the ' cuddly' experience!

Whatever you spontaneously said in childhood, may contain seeds that can be sown in adulthood! The actual job might not be *"raise puppies"!* Yet often even unrecognized to ourselves, we may express a common thread, a theme even back in early childhood, that sets the stage for a future, real-world profession, in ways more ways than you might imagine, as you read ahead in this book.

Your life dreams may even have been expressed as a ' big picture,' with various images in that photo! *'I'd love to have two children, the spouse of my dreams, and I want to raise pedigree show dogs on a big farm."* Your *dream* may be that of a dream *life!* ' Your picture of the future may be more encompassing than one factor. It may represent a number of wishes, all packaged up into one gift of the life you hope to live.

In Ecclesiastes we read, *"To everything, there is a season, and a time for every purpose under Heaven."*

In your *season* of childhood, let's say you wanted to be a pirate, and your goal in life was to explore the wild seas in a big wooden clipper ship! You wore a hat, and carried a spy glass in your hand. You liked to hold your hand over your eyes and gaze out at the sea, when you went to the beach. You pretended you could see forever, way beyond the horizon.

Today, the more mature and wiser 'you,' may still hold onto that dream! Do you love sailing? In the summer is your favorite place the beach? Do you still get that childhood feeling of '*I'm where I want to be'!* or' *This is me!*' when you are near the water?

Your dream to be a pirate, to explore the seas, from childhood, might not be as buried as you'd think. That dream may even, lead you to your very own *Treasure.* The trick is to find, and create, for yourself, the map that takes you there!

The Treasure Chest of Your Life Dreams

As an adult, you may realize you're not sure how to get there, however. "*Where's the map? How long would it take? Would I be able to survive the journey? Is there anybody else who would come with me to help? What if I DID find the Treasure?* "

As exciting as these ideas may be, the next thought that probably will pop into your head is, '*These are children's fantasies. Now I have to get back to the grind of my adult life, like it or not.* '

But lurking behind that practical statement, might be something else - hidden away, sounding like this '*I'll Never Find the Treasure. It Can't Be Done.*"

Today, you may continue to have dreams, and likely there are dreams you still hold onto, that are not yet fulfilled! As an adult, you may feel you have a greater sense, a more practical understanding, of what's involved in fulfilling the wishes or passions you hold. Perhaps you feel that ' realistically,' you can't fulfill a dream you have for who and what you'd like to be. But let's look more closely at that about change, that you feel you can't go after your dreams? Perhaps you feel *'It's a jungle out there, too much competition, too much chaos, I could get eaten alive pursuing my dream!'* ' What would happen if you took your passions and dreams for your life seriously and set forth to walk down a new pathway in life? Do you think that you would feel differently if this new pathway were to actually work out?

Fulfilling our dreams can at times feel as scary as *not* fulfilling them! Perhaps you feel that it's too scary to try!

So, your list in the morning when you wake up, does NOT include ' I think I need to change the path my life is on... starting today.' That may feel like far too big a task, and... what if it doesn't work?

Life changes often involve going ahead and moving from facing the questions you have, to taking the risk, and changing what you are both willing- and wanting- to encounter when you wake up each day. Are you a person who wants to risk all, and make enormous changes tomorrow? Or a person who tends to like to take life one step at a time? Each person is of a different temperament when it comes to taking risks, making changes in life. Do you weather rocky situations well? Are you a bold adventurer into new and unknown territories? Or do you tend to want to take a more cautious, yet steady, route? There is no ' right' or ' wrong' about people's personalities with regard to risk and change tolerance. Yet, *know thyself,* is an important part of preparing for your life journey ahead. The poet John Ruskin once said:

> *"Sunshine is delicious, rain is refreshing, wind braces us, snow is exhilarating; there is no such thing as bad weather, only different kinds of good weather."*
>
> *~ John Ruskin*

Taking the Wild Leap off a Cliff!
An Imaginary Exercise:

Imagine you are on mountain cliff, and you look down, the rocks and the rapids below are scary. If you close your eyes, you hear the loud rush of the torrential waters below. One part of you has an urge to leap. The other part of you says, "No! These waters are unknown! There could be sharp rocks! Nobody has taken this leap from where I am standing!" So, you decide not to leap. You stay safe. Sure, you have not moved from the spot where you are holding your ground on the cliff. As you open your eyes, you are back in your room, and all is familiar. The scary rapids recede. The noise subsides. Yet - here's the catch! Your urge to take that leap is still inside of you!

The Guided Path:
A Second Imaginary Exercise

You still want a change, a new experience in life You've decided against the risky leap where none have ever gone before. But what about a journey that others have explored, too? There will be a few guideposts along the way. You can imagine at a spot that goes uphill another person might even have posted a sign, 'Uphill ahead, keep going!' And at another spot where the path takes a turn, you might see a sign, 'Go left here and you'll come to the next road quickly, ' and ' Go right here but the path is slower to get to your destination.' When people have taken paths and explored what life may have to offer, frequently they want to share what they have learned.

If you close your eyes, on this guided path, how do you feel? There are colors, perhaps, sounds, fragrances, people, events, new and exciting moments to discover. Yet here is a journey that is eventful, unknown to you, but you are able to avoid the bigger dangers. This is a different type of leap! You still venture into the *unknown* - for *you*! Does this guided pathway perhaps feel challenging, exciting, but a little less dangerous than the impulsive leap? Opening your eyes, take stock of how you feel. Less fear? More adventure? Less danger? If so, then perhaps a guided journey, instead of a wild leap into unknown torrents, is more your style for the future ahead, and the road you may choose for yourself.

The Guided Journey on the Road Ahead

What the sages and wise people through the ages remind us, is that you will find mentors and guides on your new pathway. They'll offer big clues, little clues, to help you. And you yourself will be a contributor. Did you find a nice shade tree as you were walking? You may end up telling someone else, *'You are on your way! I know there's a resting spot ahead!'* Or, *"When I was your age..." and "Trust me, it's easier ahead..."*

As you discover a new path in life, if you look to the right, and to the left, and ahead and behind, you'll discover you're not completely alone. Fellow travelers are around you, and though your path is unique, you'll be able to share with each other what you are learning.

Life certainly is filled with challenges, and with fearful moments. Let's see if looking more closely at what you dream and what your passions are, can be moved into the light of day, and out of the fearful shadows. How can you examine your dreams and passions, and look at ways to move towards a more fulfilling life pathway?

In the lyrics to the song, *"You'll Never Walk Alone,"* from a musical, *"Carousel,"* written by Rogers and Hammerstein are these words of inspiration. Carousel was written during World War II, a time of great despair. During times of change, when questions abound, it takes courage to hold onto your dreams!

"When you walk through a storm, hold your head up high, and don't be afraid of the dark. At the end of the storm, is a golden sky, and the sweet silver song of a lark. Walk on through the wind, walk on through the rain, tho' your dreams be tossed and blown. Walk on, walk on, with hope in your heart, and you'll never walk alone. You'll never walk alone."

- Rogers and Hammerstein, "Carousel"

Big Dreams from Small (and bold) Steps

At any time in life, the steps one takes to create change can be small in actual size, but the momentous changes that may result, can be enormous. You may want to take small steps, but perhaps with those steps, you will see very big results. Resistance from others may enter the picture, but this is often the case when anybody makes a change that looks as though there might be a ' ripple effect.' Your friends and family may be encouraging you to make changes! Perhaps it is to take classes towards a degree, qualify for a better job, earn higher pay, or take a stand on something that is important to you. Perhaps you have support in your surroundings as you are thinking of how you will choose your direction in life from now forward. Or, on the other hand, you may be aware that there will be resistance ahead. Maybe your sister or brother is jealous of you. Maybe you know you'll have to 'tighten your belt' or get a second job in order to afford tuition. Perhaps the changes you want to create in your life will involve not just wonderful immediate results, but long hours of work and commitment to see the impact later. You may feel a combination of support, and also resistance, in your life environment. Even if you were to do nothing, take no steps at all, other than how you are living today, your future would not necessarily be absolutely secure, however. The times change. Jobs change, people's lives change, and the future itself changes before our very eyes. Hoping to not participate in the future - well, it's difficult to do that. So, looking ahead, with courage, is certainly a good option.

In 1955, a seamstress working in a department store in Montgomery, Alabama, decided to follow a dream of her own and of many people. After thoughtful contemplation, consultation with guides and mentors, and with the knowledge that what she was about to do, would be a small step in an actual physical sense, but in a symbolic sense, enormous- and life- changing - Rosa went ahead with her decision. Today she is known for the change that Rosa Parks made in her own life, that ultimately changed the lives of millions of others. Montgomery, Alabama was segregated in the 1950s. African-Americans and Whites had to sit in different places on the bus, and there were whites-only and what was then derogatively termed ' colored only' restaurants, schools, and different sections that were segregated in movie theaters and all public locations. This included the public bus. Rosa Parks, however, made a small, and very bold change. One day, she chose, with great clarity of purpose and mind, to refuse to it at the back of the bus, and to act as an equal with the white people on the bus. Rosa Parks personally challenged the South's segregation rules by her decision to take a new step in her life journey.

Rosa Parks, has gone down in history for helping to start the Civil Rights movement in the United States. Rosa Parks was walking through a storm. She chose to follow her life journey and go a route that was an uncommon one, in search of a better life. She raised a standard for her own life, and did it with much courage. Rosa was a highly thoughtful individual, aware of the importance of starting things small, and taking one step at a time. In speaking with others, Rosa Parks offered this encouragement:

"Today's mighty oak was once a nut that held its ground!"

- Rosa Parks

As the South African leader Nelson Mandela said, in a quote from the start of this Chapter, *"There is no passion to be found playing small – in settling for a life that is less than the one you are capable of living."*

This 'little' book is a guide to helping you to think 'big' about your life. In these pages, you are encouraged to dwell upon your interests, passions and choices. These encouragements are written in order to help you to find guides along the way. For, by helping you to build strong, practical bridges you'll figure out how to follow and live your passions. As you discover how to forge your next steps in life, at times, others may tell you that it is wrong to follow your dreams, that you are becoming "too big for your britches," or making others feel threatened by the fact that their lives may change as yours does! Change that is ultimately very positive, forward moving, and important in an individual's life, may be met with resistance. However, knowing that you are being true to yourself, and you are not out to do harm to others, but to have the freedom to grow, will help you to stand your ground.

If a person decides upon no life changes, perhaps striving hard to suppress a desire to change, then instead of reaching out towards the future, the future arrives anyway. The poet Henry Wadsworth Longfellow said, "*Tomorrow is the mysterious, unknown guest.*" We may not walk outside the door, but nonetheless, the future arrives, and with it, either a day of horizons that are exciting and new, or a life that you may feel is, while less fulfilling to you, more habitual.

As the ancient philosopher Lao Tzu said, observing people's changes in life, if you try to keep still, not move, then the day after tomorrow may be similar to today, and to yesterday He said:

> *"That which remains quiet is easy to handle. That which has not yet developed is easy to manage."*
>
> - *Lao Tzu, 6th C., B.C.*

You may feel you want a new road in your life, but you are not sure if the changes may be too much to handle. What would others think? If you went on your life journey, and it took you to college, or a new career, or to a new city, meeting new people-what would happen to the past, where you've already been? It may be that you cannot hold onto the past exactly as it was, and turn this into the future. You may be surprising yourself, in even thinking ahead into the future! Yet everyone harbors images of the future, even if a few days, or weeks or months ahead. What those images are, and what relationship the future bears to your past, and to the present, is for you to decide. Indeed, two writers, Marge Piercy and Grace Paley, showed their different approaches to the future. Marge Piercy wrote a book entitled, Small _Changes,_ and Grace Paley wrote a book entitled, _Enormous Changes at the Last Minute._

Chapter Two

Discovering Your Life Passions

—⟋⟍—

*"Choose a job you love and
you will never have to work a day in your life."*

- Confucius

"I would rather die of passion than of boredom."

-Vincent van Gogh

How Do I Figure Out My Life Passions?

"How do I get there?" may be the question you have in your mind right now! Let's look at the question that comes before that! Hold on! Take a little step back! Before asking how to get there, you may want to go right ahead and ask the question that is the most tempting one to skip over! *"How do I figure out what my life passions are?"* This may feel self-evident to you, or you may have to dig down to discover the *Buried Treasure of Your Life Dreams.*

You may have a 'sense' of what your real life dreams are. That's a great starting point! So, how can this 'intuition' of what you wish for your life, become a reality? How do you bring the picture into clearer focus, so you can see it up close? How do you find the 'X marks the spot' of your Life Dreams, if you're not exactly sure where the path to this discovery begins?

Moving From "Maybe" to "Yes"!!

Figuring out what you feel pretty confident you want to do on the next portion of your life journey, will be an important first step. Moving from 'well I'm pretty sure ' to 'yes, I'm sure' is a good starting point. Then, finding out how to get there, is the next step. There are smaller steps to these bigger stepping stones, too, along the way. While a dream may feel like the story is complete, the day-to-day of our lives is a work-in-progress. Making a dream a reality takes creativity, and commitment. The third 'c' is compassion. Be kind to yourself. Even the Creator needed time to build the world. Your life design may take a little more time than you might wish. Our dreams don't always hand us the magic wand for daily miracles. Yet there are many steps which, if you take them, will help you to be a builder of your dreams.

The playwright Lorraine Hansberry, who spent a lifetime striving towards her dream to become a professional writer for the theater, and succeeded, said, "Never be afraid to sit awhile and think,"

The design you create will be both practical, and fulfilling. An important goal is for you to make a toolkit for designing the future you want to create for your life. Think about and identify your interests. Then, we'll move on to look at how can you show others what you love to do, by developing skills. Building upon what do you already know you're good at, you'll design a plan. What do you want to be better at doing? Who and what can help you to reach your highest potential? And not only 'how,' but 'when'? From a dream to a practical timeline for mapping and taking the journey may seem a big leap. When you wake up in the morning, you do something even bigger than that. Every day, you wake up and you are alive. From that gift you have been given, and the gift of dreams, you can create a life that you will feel honored to wake up to, every day.

Choosing 'What' You Want to Do - and Planning Ahead!

How do you draw upon what's 'feasible' and what you're passionate about - both - to lead the life you want to live? Those questions can be asked - and answered- together! Let's look at a few steps you can take that are 'inner' - inside of you - and 'outer' - specific activities you can accomplish in the external environment, in order to bring what is ' practical' for your life, together with what your life 'passions' are - now, and into the future. This doesn't have to be a long, 'forever wait' to take steps towards a more fulfilling, exciting, happier life! You can start today, with steps that you choose. These can be large - or they can be small. All steps lead somewhere. The important thing is - you are deciding what to do with your life, and moving toward your dreams. Standing still is one way to decide. It means, however, that you aren't making a choice to change. What if you did make changes in your life? While that very idea may fill you with apprehension - look down the road - farther - a little farther, even, than that... and what do you see? Your life as it is now? Or your life - improved, happier, more enriched, each and every day?

Loving what you do, and being good at it, that's a combination which leads to more than a job. Passion plus skill = fulfillment. Combining "What I love' with ' What my skills are' can change life's journey profoundly. There's a third vital factor to the equation, too. ' What's unique about me, special to me, to my character, my talents- to who I am?' This sacred third element is your uniqueness as a human being.

A book is a guide, but it isn't 'the answer,' in itself. That is found within your heart, and your mind, as you combine your passions and your choices. The goal is to point these out to you, by asking you to look more closely at what you love, and what you want to accomplish in your life.

Based upon this book, you'll make your choices on your journey for the weeks, and months ahead in your life. When you reach another set of important decisions, you can then look at this guide again, and you may find your own answers have changed. Every turning point in life offers new choices in following your passions.

Identifying Your Talents and Skills

Let's start first with delving into YOU! What are your life passions? How do you feel about your talents? Claiming your talents and skills is an important element of being who you are. How do you enrich the world for others? For yourself? Exploring yourself is a challenge! The creativity of self-insight leads to many rewards.

Let's start with looking at YOU. Who are you today, right now?

Chapter Three

Your Work Can Be Your Dream!

—ww—

Your Personal Life Interview!

Have you ever been interviewed before? Thinking about and talking about one's own life may seem ' easy,' but when it comes right down to it, you need to 'let go of appearances,' and get to the heart of the matter - that is - to your own heart! Let's go! Have you ever 'interviewed yourself'? No? Well!! Hang onto your hat!! You're going to delve in this next section, into the heart of what matters - to you!!

You probably have been ' interviewed' but perhaps without calling it that. Let's say a new friend is getting to know you! Perhaps a relative you haven't seen in a long while is 'catching up' with you about your life. Or, an employer is wanting to know more about you in a job interview! Maybe in your synagogue, or in a family get-together, you are asked, "How are you these days? What are you doing? What do you like to do? What are your interests?"

Ok! Well, you are now embarking upon a new and different type of interview! You get to talk, so to speak, and to view and listen to yourself - both sides of the mirror! You are doing the asking - and answering!

You are going to be the Interviewer and also the' Subject of your Life Interview!

Enjoy! Explore! There's no microphone! Your audience consists of one person! Your external speaker volume is down low! You can say whatever you wish! Nobody has to hear! Just - You! Therefore, be as candid as you wish to be - with yourself!! This is your time, your heart, and your 'calling' - to be - yourself!

The Life Interview

Listening to Your Goals and Dreams

Creating Your Questions!

To help you to identify your strengths, let's look at a particular approach that can be fun and challenging: The Life Interview! Here are questions to get you started! Then, you can create your own Life Interview Questions, including these, and more that you will discover! Feel free to answer these questions-for yourself, to yourself! Have fun! Guess what? There's a good chance you are going to surprise yourself!!

Let's start with the Life Interview questions here, and then you will very likely find other questions that YOU will create, to ask yourself! Explore! There's no right or wrong answer! You - that's the answer to all questions here! You, as you are living your life.

Life Interview Question #1

What types of skills do people turn to you for? This may be among family and friends, or at work or school. What are you known for?

One way to approach this question might be to think about what do friends, neighbors, community members, co-workers, tend to turn to you for? Do people, for example, turn to you for advice when there's a conflict with a family member? Are you a peace-keeper and a peace-seeker? Are you a good listener? Are you a practical person? Do you ' fix' broken things? Are you a good organizer? Are you the person who figures out the grocery bill? Are you the cousin who remembers all the family birthdays? What do you do, that you like to do? There doesn't have to be a reason why you like doing what you do! What's important is that you like it!! And, perhaps, other people may notice this, and call upon you for your skills. What might some of these be, even if YOU don't consider this to be a skill, an interest, a talent, it is likely that other people have recognized you, in little, or big, ways. What do they notice? What do you notice that other people notice - about you?

As an example: Your neighbor has constant troubles with his computer. He is always in need of help - a virus scan, a program installation, trouble-shooting. He calls you, ' Would you mind helping me again? Thanks so much!'

An employer calls you in, because a co-worker is ill, and you are great with customers. You are asked to take the front reception desk for the week, to be the person who ' represents the company' when the public walks in the door. The company has 30 employees! Who was asked to meet and greet, because you are friendly and skillful at it? You!!

A neighborhood community center gives you a call. Last year, you volunteered in the soup kitchen, and the people who showed up have been asking for that 'great woman who was here last year... ' to organize the holiday dinner. You pulled off such a wonderful dinner for everybody! Could you help out again this year?

Or, you have discovered, all on your own, by yourself, without anybody knowing, that you have a memory for names and faces. You can meet twenty people at a get-together, and say ' hello' to each of them for only a few minutes. Somehow, you recall all of the details about each person - everything spoken, and the qualities of each individual. You have a great memory. On top of that, you're a people-person!

Perhaps it is something that nobody notices, but that you notice. What are you aware of, about your life activities and interests, that other people may not even know about?

Are you the person who, at the pedestrian crosswalk, waits at the corner to cross, and then walks with the eldest person crossing the street, just to give that person company? Are you the person who stops at the light, gets out of your car, and picks up the styrofoam cup that is sitting in the middle of the street? Are you the humorist at work who keeps everybody in a good mood during the day? Are you the person who stays late, just to make sure that the lights are out and the copy machine is off? Do you find you are the one who organizes the neighborhood bake-a-thon, fundraiser, the mini-marathon, or the annual summer trip to the beach, for the kids on the block? What do you do, just 'because' you like to do this? What are your ' feel good' moments during the day?

Take out a piece of paper, and write down whatever comes to mind! It may seem not of importance - to anybody - except you!!! That's fine! Write it down! Is it an interest? A specific activity? A way doing things? What you do every day that's just ' part of who you are?' Go ahead, write it down!

You may not define what you are writing on your list as 'talents' - it may be that you feel this is 'you' and nothing special. Here's the first myth we'll bust open! Are you thinking ' Well, these little elements of my life aren't very noteworthy.' Everything About You Is Noteworthy!! The Life Interview is all about you, in great detail!

So, write down whatever comes to mind, as you think about the question above!! Explore! Enjoy!

Life Interview Question #2:

What do you know about your own 'style' of work and learning, that others may not know about you?

Here's a self-discovery! You have found that you are a late-night person who loves to work ' solo.' You do your best work, in the evenings, with nobody else around. You are friendly! You're not anti-social! But you are very self-motivated and you like to get the job done, on your own time, in your own way! You are a great self-starter, and very inner-motivated!

Another self discovery- you are skilled in remembering music! You've noticed that if somebody hums a tune; you remember it easily! When you listen to the radio, you can sing each tune 'by heart' with no problem! If somebody plays music on the piano, later you can ' pick out the notes' without much effort. You are musically gifted! Where other people may just enjoy an afternoon walk, you walk, and hum, and notice sounds all around you! Music is your thing!

Here's a different self-discovery When you are cleaning and organizing in your home, you have found it's fun to create 'systems' for organization! You have organized your books by author. You've created extra space in your cabinets by stacking like items. You've labeled bins on the shelves for your home office. When friends are disorganized and cluttered, you can right away see what will help them! You have organizational skills!

Another self-discovery! Your neighbor has a dog that goes crazy in the elevator. Every time the little dog steps into the elevator, the dog cries, yelps, runs around, and is generally in a panic! The neighbor has no idea what to do. But guess what? You've discovered you're a 'dog whisperer!' You say and do all the right things, and the little dog calms right down. After a week of 'elevator training,' the little dog is nice and calm in the elevator! You have found that you have a way with animals.

Life Interview Question #3:

What are you known for on your job? What types of skills have come to the foreground, for which you have been recognized? If you know you have these skills, and people haven't yet noticed - what would you LIKE to be recognized for?

Looking over the last quarter of your company's earnings, and its areas where profits declined, too, you have identified three ways in which earnings could be improved by streamlining manufacturing processes. You have written up a report on this, and given it to your boss. Your boss asked you to present it at the shareholders' meeting next month! Good for you! Your boss has recognized you have excellent skills in understanding the business structure!

Last month, in your school, the children were really going wild at recess. Nobody could control them, and there were fights on the playground. You're a social studies teacher. You decided that you'd create a playground activity - a map of the U.S.A! In teams, the kids identified the State Capitals! Everybody was running around to stand on the Capital cities before the other team could get there! Mayhem? No! Organizational fun? Yes! Your School Principal thanked you and now "State Capitals" have become part of the class recess! What a relief! And this is due to your idea! You are a creative thinker!! You're great with kids! You are a natural team leader!

Life Interview Question #4:

If you were to describe a skill you feel you could teach others, what would it be?

Last week, Susie and Jim, two children in their teens, who are your friends' kids, could not figure out how to install the new brakes on Jim's bicycle. You went to visit the family, and there in the garage, was Jim's bicycle. The tire was off. No brakes. The kids were in despair. The weekend was going to be dismal. So, you sat down with them, wrench in hand, and you replaced the brakes. You also showed Jim how to do the brake replacement. On the front brakes, you did the installation. You explained every step and showed them how. Then Jim replaced the back brakes. What do you think? Could you teach bike repair? YES!!

In the past few months, you took a free course at the library, in teaching English to immigrants. You were given reading materials, and you did practice sessions that were observed. You studied the teaching methods, and over 3 months, you learned to break down the steps to teaching verbs, adverbs, nouns, and grammar to people with little English background. You have discovered that you can teach a language.

Last week, you had a phone call from a relative. A close neighbor had passed away. Your cousin wanted to help out with the funeral arrangements, but didn't know the first thing to do. You realized help was needed. You jumped in, made lists of relatives, contacted the funeral home, set the schedule, organized the gathering at the family home, got food, and set up the tables and reception area. You talked with the family, asked them what they wanted, and became the facilitator. You did this intuitively, with empathy, and a sense of what was needed. You also organized well. You have discovered you can stay calm in a stressful emotional situation, and that you can help others. A week later, one of the family members called you. Could you sit down and go over how you'd put everything together? They were so grateful, and you did such a good job, they'd like to understand how you did it and want to thank you. You sit down with them, and find that you can describe how you put things together, and what you thought about. This helped them to feel that they had more understanding, and also, closure. You were the ' do-er' and then, the teacher.

Life Interview Question #5:

What do you do well around the house?

Well, you've decided to make a time grid! What do you do around the house each week? As it turns out, you do a lot! You organize the recycling. You get the groceries. You do the dishes after dinners. You get the kids to bed by 8 PM. You schedule the lawn mowing. You organize the neighborhood Spring Planting. You do the homework with the kids. You are the Girl Scout organizer for the local Girl Scouts. Guess what? You are a superb multi-tasker! And, you encourage others to do their part, as well! The kids grumble, but they DO take out the garbage! The dog DOES get fed! The laundry DOES get folded and back in everybody's rooms! These activities help life run smoothly! And who is the organizer of all of this? Gosh! It's you!

Life Interview Question #6:

What Have You Been Happiest Doing in Your Life?

Okay, let's take a trip back in time! Remembering as far back as you can, when were you happiest doing what you were doing? Was it that time when you went camping, and you spent 4 weeks outdoors in nature, in a tent? (You live in a big city!)

Was it when you were working at a local cafe, and organizing the weekly soup menu? You went and found the ingredients, did the local sourcing, and created the menu. You taught the kitchen staff how to make the soups, and asked the customers which ones they liked best! You loved it!

What about that time when you went with your cousin to a local technology exhibition? You were in seventh heaven looking at all the ' future' technologies that are to come in the next 50 years! You could imagine the future, and not only that, a few inventions that you didn't see at the technology fair- the ones in your head! Since then, you've been reading about Leonardo da Vinci!

What about the time when you took the bus to work every day, instead of the train, and you worked closer to home? You got to know your co-workers better. You could even socialize with them on the weekends, because you all lived nearby. You got home earlier from work. It was so nice, to have a local job, and be close to home.

Or, perhaps it was one winter when your aunt had to go to a clinic to help her with physical therapy. You accompanied her. You got to know the other patients, and you sat and talked with people. You had time away from a job that was isolating, sitting alone at a desk. You really enjoyed the 'team' spirit' of the clinic. You discovered that you like that environment - team work.

Was it when you were reading to your nieces and nephews, just before their bedtime? You read the children's stories aloud, with different accents, and the kids loved it, and so did you!!

When have you felt most relaxed, happiest, in your life? Was it with a newfound acquaintance? Was it when starting a new school? A new relationship? Perhaps it was on your 20th Wedding Anniversary! Or maybe, it was just yesterday, walking down the street, noticing the sun, the birds, and the sky. Did you feel, at that moment - happy? Relaxed? Very much alive?

- Think about it.
- What makes you happy?
- What do you love to do?
- What do people know you for?
- What do you know yourself for?
- These questions are ways to get to know a very important person in your life.
- That person is YOU.
- Guess what? This little book is not done without YOU!!
- Next up? Creative brainstorming - all about YOU!!

Life Interview Question #7:

What In Your Wildest Dreams Would You Love To Do?

If you think about it, you have probably had many moments in life in which you have enjoyed the people you were surrounded by, the community you were living in, and the job you were doing. You enjoyed friends, and family.

If you think further into that ' life picture,' whether from the distant past, or the recent past, there are very likely elements of that 'picture,' that you can identify as being important to the ' why' and the 'how' of that time. Looking at those key components can help you to figure out what you like, what makes you happiest, what you are most passionate about.

A feeling you may have, too, rooted deeply in the human spirit, is a yearning -for what hasn't yet been. For what might be. What do you dream of? What do you imagine for your life? What do you hope for, in your innermost dreams? Perhaps you've not even yet admitted this to yourself! You may never have even mentioned it to other people! Did you feel that it could never happen? Was it simply out of reach? A dream that could never-come-true?

If you may have felt at times in your life, ' Yes, the past was fine... but things could be much better, even great... ' then maybe you haven't yet brought your deepest dreams into view, even spoken them aloud- to yourself.

Or, even, as many people feel in life 'Well, if I'm really honest, the past hasn't been that great. There were years, months, days, in which I've felt OK. But there were many times when I've struggled. I've felt unhappy. I've not known what to do. I've been in life situations that were hard for me, and I didn't want to remain in those situations. I definitely needed to change my life.' Maybe that's how you feel, right now.

Looking at your dreams - doesn't hurt. It can really help. Your dreams are a part of you. Your dreams can help you to see who and what you really want to be. You may have a 'big dream' that you feel you can do, in parts! Dreams don't have to come true 'all at once.' Dreams certainly don't need to be 'now or never.' They may very well be, 'One step at time.' Until you know the dream, and can look at it directly, without fear, without anxiety, you'll never know what steps you need to take to make your dreams come true.

Why be afraid of a dream? Maybe it seems as though *that's not me,*' or ' *nobody would understand,*' or *'it's too difficult,*' or ' *how could I possibly learn that?*' Dreams aren't meant to hold us back. Dreams are meant to help us to move forward in our lives. We learn from dreams. They are there for a reason. They help us to become all of ourselves - our true selves, our best selves, and our highest selves. God would not have given us dreams, if we weren't meant to learn from them, and to become our dreams.

The writer Kurt Vonnegut once said, "*We become what we believe.*" This includes what we believe about ourselves, our roles in life, and whether our dreams can, indeed, become our realities.

Leonardo da Vinci Dreamt of Flight! How About You?

When Leonardo da Vinci dreamt of flying through the sky in a flying machine - the mechanical structure of the machine did not yet exist. He did not have the detailed information about wind shear, loft, and aerodynamics that would have helped him to make a flying machine. This did not stop him from dreaming, and from looking at clues in the world around him to see whether there were already signs and roadmaps for how to go from the earth into the sky. Lo and behold- the birds of nature were able to help show him the way. By taking on little birds as his guides, Leonardo was able to observe how they gained loft, speed, turned, and landed. He found guides and learned from them, even though neither species could speak the language of the other. Leonardo dreamed beyond his time, of a world in the future. Though the ease with which little birds could fly might have made him wonder if humans could ever do what they did so effortlessly, he kept trying to surpass his own knowledge.

We all have many dreams! Looking at the range of your dreams, which ones are you happy to keep as dreams or fantasies about life? Which ones do you want to make come true? Differentiating among your dreams can definitely help in figuring out how to take the steps to make certain dreams come true. The wishful, fun dreams are great to have! They help us to keep our imaginations alive!! You might say to yourself, ' *I wish I could live back in the 19th century when people traveled by horse and* buggy!" Or you might wish, *"Wouldn't it be great to be able to fly into the future? I hope we can do time-travel and then I can visit a 1000 years from now- in advance!"* These wishful dreams are explorations of the mind that can lead to big inventions! Think of Leonardo da Vinci, and his 'flying machine' made of wood and paper, compared to today's jet airplane! Or think of Galileo's little, handheld telescope, with a fuzzy, hand-ground lens, compared to the giant, precision, digitally-tracking Hubble telescope today! The big dreams help all of humanity to evolve. Your big dreams may well become part of the age of invention in the 2lst century! So, hang onto them, and foster them, and help the big dreams to grow!

While dreaming of places faraway or invisible worlds, the life that you are blessed to have, is the one that can often be the best ' time and place' for you. Living your life in the present, and looking to the past and future to help guide you, may be the way to 'live' your most ' doable' dreams. These are the dreams you have that can come true, in your lifetime, day to day, from a tiny germ of an idea, to a reality! What are the doable dreams you have? They may be small and easy to accomplish, or larger, and take more time. Either way, if you make a plan, create a map, you can find your way from dreams, to reality.

Doable Dreams

Do you want to learn to drive? Ok, there's a goal that you can do, it is reachable, and doable. Do you want to learn how to type?

Definitely, you can. Do you want to learn how to speak another language? Yes, add that to the 'list of your life goals. It may be tempting to just concentrate on the smaller goals that feel like they are more ' doable.' *"I can mow the lawn this afternoon, no problem."* *"Can I learn Spanish today?"* OK, perhaps not all at once. *"I can read Chapter One in my Introduction to Spanish book today!"* There is a doable step. Let's consider in greater depth, what might happen in your life, if you were to first, believe in your dreams, and second, take the steps that move your dreams from a wish - into a reality.

Chapter Four

Mapping Your New Life Direction

—ᴡᴡ—

The Small Steps to the Big Leap!

By now you're probably adding up those individual moments when you've been able to be of help, when your skills were useful, when others recognized that you had particular talents that were helpful, and when you saw this for yourself, too! These are real-world, everyday events, in which you applied yourself, and results took place. You noticed. Others noticed. You realized, ' *Hey, here's something I can do well!'*

Have you noticed, too, that you may have been asked not only once or twice, even ten times, or more, to help with organizing a party, a family function, a food drive, a local Spring clean-up....? People have started to realize that ' organizing' is your talent! And you have started to notice, these are not 'one-time' or isolated requests! You have been called upon more than once, for specific talents and skills! You've recognized these talents and skills, that exist not just once in awhile, but all the time, inside yourself!   This realization is a very important one.

Making Your Own Guide to Your Future

The talents you have are not 'here for a minute, then gone.' These persist. They are intrinsic to you; they are a part of who you are as a person. Over time, if you focus on developing these skills, they become of high value to others- to the world around you, and can lead, if you wish, to professional goals and achievements. What takes you, however, from ' *I am good at this...*' to ' *I have a job doing this...*'? Interests you have found you return to time and again, often point you in a positive direction for the future. Making a guide to your future doesn't usually mean abandoning your past! It often means looking to your own life interests and history, and figuring out what you want to do that is part of the past, and also takes you into the future. Your guide to the future may well be a map of your past, your present, and your future, all rolled into one.

Adding up the Parts to Make the Whole: Part I

We don't have to be mathematicians, logicians, or have a skill in measuring perspective, as Euclid did in geometry, for example, in order to realize that 'putting things in perspective' in life can often be a matter of looking at how the parts add up to the whole. Add up the various views of your future, and what do you see? What is the shape of your future, when you add up the parts of your imagined design, and look at these parts, together, as a whole?

It is said that as people we are more than the sum ' of our parts. We have a physical being, and certainly a spiritual awareness, and also emotions. We are at least three parts to the wholeness of ourselves! And likely, many more parts, too. By the same token, if you think about what you love to do, it will be 'more than just the activities' themselves. Other intrinsic factors that are not fully describable may be 'why' you love tuning up a car engine, or building a fine piece of furniture, or designing a website. If you DO add up the key components of what you like to do, there may not be a 'name' of a profession that you can neatly fit these activities into. Indeed, there may be more than one way that the pieces fit together. Figuring out the 'right fit' for you, will be adding up the sum of the parts, and seeing if you like the end result enough to make the work fit into your life plan.

Adding Up the Parts to Make a Whole: Part II

So, you're good at organizing events? Many types of jobs require strong organizational skills and understanding of ' how to get the job done.' This might range from a manufacturing plan and the workflow from one individual to the next, in product creation, to a book publishing company, and making sure manuscripts can get from draft to the finished book out in retail stores. Organizing skills might mean that you're the dispatch person for an emergency ambulance service. Organizational talents might mean that you are the Department Chair of an educational institution, organizing programs and curricula. Or, you've decided to become your own employer, and create a small business. Your business grows, and you have employees, a set of goals and tasks to accomplish, and an entire organization to run!

However, getting from the point of a realization of your talents, to being in the world doing the work you love, takes a few more steps - not just on the outside, but on the inside, especially.

There's an important step that takes you from ' I know how to do this' and "I'm good at this' - to living what you love, and living out your passions, as a part of your everyday life. What is that step? It has to do with an element of life that can be called existential! How do you see yourself? In a good way, you might even say to yourself, ' Who do you think you are?'

Adding Up the Parts to Make the Whole: Part III

So, it turns out that you write memos well at work? You helped a friend to write a cover letter for a job application? Your cousin asked you to proofread his entrance essay for college? You have noticed that the newspaper is missing a few important current events on the front page? Not only do you like to write, but you notice writing in the world around you!

Saying to yourself, '*I like to write'* is an important realization. Then, further, acknowledging, I'm good at writing,' is a second very important step. You're admitting that you have a talent!! This is cause for celebration! You are recognizing your skills, and that you do, indeed, have these skills.

These are steps that are necessary, as you gain momentum for a big leap. The big leap of faith, is going from the 'doing' of the things you like to do, to the realization that you can ' be' the things you like to do! ' *Doing and being* are closely related. They are great friends! They are similar, but not the same. *Doing* is when you are engaged in the activity itself. *"I'm writing right now."* Yet, what happens when you stop writing? You're done with one writing project! What happens next? Will you do another one?

This is where a big leap of faith from ' *I'm writing,'* to ' *I'm a writer'* takes place. Because, in between your projects, such as writing an editorial for a local paper, or a letter to your congresswoman, or a menu for a party, you do not 'stop' having the skill of ' writing.' The skill is part of you - it's part of what you do. And it is also part of who you are. So, you can take that leap, from *doing* to *being*. When you talk with other people, when you think, inside, about yourself - go ahead, and say it! Not just ' I like to write,' or ' I'm writing' but rather, *"I am a writer!"*

In the world of show business, there is a popular joke that Frank Sinatra, the famous 'crooner,' was expressing a profound life philosophy every time he sang, because he was singing: *"Do be do be do!"*

Designing Your Job from your Talents

Once you realize you can give yourself a 'name' that describes your talents, you can then let other people know, concretely, what you want to do, and what you love to do, when applying for a job. From saying to yourself and others, '*I am a writer,* ' to gaining training in school, in writing, you can then move on to, ' *Dear Sir, I am applying for a journalism job,*' - this becomes a natural step to take. But you must ' own' and 'believe' in your talents and skills, first. This makes all the difference in the world - taking that leap of faith. Or, as Sinatra put it, *"Do be do be do!"* And as the lyrics in Carousel say, ' *Hold your head up high,*" for in walking your path in life, if you are trusting and have faith in using your skills and talents, *'You'll never walk alone.'*

Identifying Your Particular Skills and Talents

Each human being on the planet has the ability to share his or her unique individuality by sharing skills and talents. You may already be sharing a number of skills and talents. You have made these' explicit' therefore - showing your skills to others! For every skill you have already shared and demonstrated, you are sure to have many abilities that are 'implicit, ' just waiting to be revealed. You can also look at how other people live out their dreams and express their talents, to help you to make decisions on your journey.

What do you enjoy seeing others do? What do you feel you could participate in, that you have not yet jumped into? Do you wish you could do a certain something, and feel that you may, indeed, be good at it? Your observations of others helps. When a person is engaged in a particular activity, do you find yourself paying very close attention, watching all the details, and even feeling that you could go through those details well, yourself? Let's say you are watching a person in your physician's office. He or she is taking someone's blood pressure, and listening to the person's heart. You see how the cuff is placed, and how the numbers are written down. You find yourself asking questions, '*How does this work? What do the numbers mean?'*

One very strong indicator of what you may yourself want to develop as a skill, is to observe what sparks your curiosity. What do you go home to and want to find out more about? What do you ask others to explain further, about something they are doing? You may well be exploring something that you yourself would like to do, expressed as a curiosity about how other people do that! Keep going with that curiosity! You can discover skills and talents you have, or wish to have, observing what you find very interesting in the work of others, and also, your hidden ' dreams' of what you want to do. Asking yourself, not only' *what are my talents,'* but *'what are my interests'* and *'what do I observe in other people's skills?'* these questions tend to go hand-in-hand, in identifying your interests in job-related or professional terms.

Translating Activities into Professions!

If you sit and take out a piece of paper, there's a very good chance you'll be able to write down at least ten things that you enjoy observing in other people's work, and that you find very interesting! Perhaps it is the entire profession itself- such as Emergency Medical Technician! Or, perhaps it's part of a job, such as "helping other people to feel better in a crisis." Maybe it's a specific activity that applies to a number of types of professions, such as "I enjoy a view from above- working off the ground!" This could apply to a construction worker, a cable installer, a telephone repair person, a pilot, a window washer, an aerial photographer - to many different professions!

Writing Down Your Interests
By Activity; By Profession

By writing down your interests into two categories, one by Profession, the other by Activity, you'll be able to see what activities may fall into more than one profession.

You can also find out what professions may have different types of activities -some of which you may enjoy, and others activities perhaps not as much.

This is a way to help you to recognize and clarify how your interests can 'translate' into more than one profession. Also, a particular profession, while appealing as a ' title,' or an ' idea,' when you break it down into the activities in that profession, can reveal more about what you'd actually do, day to day in that career. Looking closely at interests, activities, and professions can help clear away the myths and realities about what you want to do, versus what the specific profession actually offers.

Interests	Activiies	Professions
Sports	Biking	Bicycle Repair
Science	Helping Others	Nursing

Make a BIG Chart of your Interests, Activities, and the Professions that are consistent with these! Add to the chart below, to start!

Interests	Activiies	Professions

Two Imaginary Roads! Wide? or Branching?

Here is an exercise of the imagination to explore the different activities and interests you have, and where they may lead you.

Imagine a road. That road is one you are walking on. It is a beautiful road, on a gorgeous day! The road is lined with houses, flowers, trees, people, all waving and encouraging you as you are walking. This is a big, wide road. It points in one direction only. This is a pathway where you have an option to go ahead and simply walk down this pathway that leads to a single goal. Imagine what that goal is, and give it a name. It is the name of a profession. What do you see at the end of this wonderful road? Is it a sign that says ' Nursing Station' or a sign that says ' Veterinary Practice, ' or a sign that says ' High School Teacher'? What does the sign on your road say?

Then, you realize you have the option for a second, different road, if you wish to go on that road. When you explore this second road, there are, lo and behold, a number of options!! The road branches! Each branch goes in a separate direction all on its own. Do you see signs down all of these branches? Is there a sign that says, for example, 'Pharmacist,' down one branch, and 'Lab Researcher,' down another branch, and 'Home Health Aide' down a third branch? You realize these are somewhat related, they have to do with health and science. But these are very different branches. Which one do you choose? Or, are you more comfortable going back to that single wide road with only one end point, one sign?

Well, you have just explored two different ways of thinking about your future - through the focused single-path approach, or ' convergent' thinking, and the 'branching' approach, or ' divergent' thinking.

When you use 'Convergent' thinking, you are exploring a single profession, such as the work of a Firefighter, a Social Worker, a Teacher, a Retail Manager. That's the one road that keeps getting wider. There's one Profession on that road, and it has a lot to offer!

When you use "Divergent' thinking, you are looking at an 'interest, such as ' science,' and the interest branches out to a number of roads! There are many roads on the 'Divergent' thinking pathway, when you keep an interest in mind, and then ask which professions include that interest!

So, the two roads exercise above, can be very helpful, and encourages thinking creatively about your life, your interests, and your skills. You will quickly see which road is the more comfortable, more intriguing one, for you. Perhaps you are energetically, in your mind's eye, exploring all the different branches of the second road. Or, perhaps you are happily going down the first road, feeling secure that there are no other options that interest you, as you've chosen this particular path!

Taking Your Interests on a Test Drive!

We all have interests that we explore simply because we can't help ourselves!! Does local news about pets at the lost-and-found catch your eye every day in the newspaper? Do you follow when each pet is adopted, and by whom? Do you read about animal rights? Perhaps you go to help out on weekends with the ASPCA.

Are you a person who has to see every movie that a particular actor has been in? Do you love silent films? Are you a fan of historical wartime movies? Do you have a 'movie watching list' a mile long, all on one genre?

Take a look at your bookshelves! Do you have a particular 'common theme' in books you read? Are you reading science fiction a lot? Books written by a particular author? Books about cars? Books about fashion? What are your interests as seen on your bookshelves?

When you have time off, from work or from school, what do you like to do? What's your list of what you love to do to relax? Are you an outdoors person? Do you have 2 bicycles, a skateboard, and rollerblades? Are you a hiker? A kayaker? Do you like to take nature walks? Or are you someone who loves to cook, stay home, relax, and explore new recipes? Do you share ideas with others, perhaps writing a ' blog' on your computer, on a particular topic?

Make a list of your "Casual Interests"...! By casual, this represents your interests for which you are not paid, and which aren't directly part of your work or your current profession. Which interests might you wish to take on a 'test drive' down an imaginary 'career road'? Explore, drive down the various branches, and see what your imagination comes up with!

If you love to paddle a kayak on weekends, what might 'kayaking' include professionally? Options could be, for example: Adventure Guide, Retail Store Sports, Nature Photographer, Summer Camp Kayaking with Children.

Are there any of your "Casual Interests' you might even combine? This is where brainstorming can get to be fun and interesting! Your divergent roads might converge! The branches might meet! What about Kayaking and Cooking? Might there be work that combines the two? What about a 'niche catering company' 'Lunch in the Sun" - a picnic catering service! Or what about, for example, "Bicycles and Writing" as two of your interests?

While it is tempting in thinking about your interests in separate, divided in categories, taking your interests all together on a ' test drive' (it's a big convertible!) can help you to brainstorm and see how the various interests you have may 'converge' from different branches, into a hybrid interest!

Go Ahead! The Road that Says "My Road!"

Many times, thinking about what you might do in life, you may encounter a wonderful wish! Perhaps it is a 'dream job' you have thought about! Or, you know you have a certain skill, but you think, ' *Well, it's nice to have fun with this, but it's just an interest, I have to get serious about my life! I have to find a serious job!'* Having work that pays well, and a profession that you love, does not require that you be miserable and suffer! If you think about an interest, a skill, and then, a job you'd love to have, does the next thought that comes to mind, sound like this? *"That's not me!"* Or ' *That can't be me!"*

Imaginary Exercise: The Life Thruway

Imagine yourself driving or walking down a very active, major road. There are many "on ramps" and there are "exit ramps." The road also has a number of options - there are roads that come and go and branch out from the "*Life Thruway.*" You are very excited to be on this road! However, there's a problem. Every time you come to a branch, you have to choose where to go. That part is exciting! But, when you look ahead, a sign appears that says, *'Don't Enter Here! Danger!'* *'Construction Underway'* and *'No Entrance!'*

There's a Construction Manager, and that person, as it happens, is you.

The problem with saying to yourself, at each possibility that shows up in life, *'That's not me!"* is the *"Life Thruway"* starts to become blocked. The road ahead reads, not just *'Construction Underway'* but then there's a little sign that you yourself have created, as the Construction Manager! And that little sign reads *"PS. You Just Have to Stop Here. Construction Ahead is Forever. Sorry."*

The Life Thruway has a construction problem, if it turns out, that not a single road ahead is one you can imagine yourself on. Then, you can't go anywhere.

Who is Managing the Road Construction?

There's good news, however! You are the Construction Manager!! You can change the Construction Signs!! Let's see if you can try out a different reply! What about saying, instead of `That Can't be Me'* at every fork in the road, you ask yourself, *'Could That be Me?"* You've decided to open up a few exit signs, and a few branches, and even create a new main road, if you wish. The road construction is all yours to decide.

If, when you think about what you'd love to do, and then say to yourself, *"That could be me!"* all of a sudden, new the roads appear in life, that you can explore!! When you say *"This could be my road!"* That very thought can lead to major new pathways in life!!

The *Life Thruway* you are constructing receives your own go-ahead! As Construction Manager, you can authorize miles and miles of wonderful, new, exciting roads to be created ahead! Not only do you get to name these roads, but you get to decide when they'll be built, where, by what means, and which ones you yourself want to personally travel upon! Not only that, but the *Life Thruway* has plenty of room for fellow travelers!

Let's look at the *Road You Decide To Build*, next.

The Road Not Taken

Two roads diverged in a yellow wood,

And sorry I could not travel both

And be one traveler, long I stood

And looked down one as far as I could

To where it bent in the undergrowth;

Then took the other, as just as fair,

And having perhaps the better claim,

Because it was grassy and wanted wear;

Though as for that the passing there

Had worn them really about the same,

And both that morning equally lay

In leaves no step had trodden black.

Oh, I kept the first for another day!

Yet knowing how way leads on to way,

I doubted if I should ever come back.

I shall be telling this with a sigh

Somewhere ages and ages hence:

Two roads diverged in a wood, and I—

I took the one less traveled by,

And that has made all the difference.

- Poet, Robert Frost

Your Roadmaps! Charting the Course

Here is a Roadmap Chart #1 that can help you to think about combining your interests, skills, and a future job. How about brainstorming, no matter how far-fetched it may sound to you! Try your hand below, and make a bigger chart of your own to keep going! You may find that *more than one job* will fit the combination of your interests and skills! Even if you fill just 'My Interests' at first, then you can add skills you'd like to learn, to gain the job you wish to have. Keeping ongoing Roadmap Charts can help you to explore how to get from where you are now, to where you want to be.

Roadmap Chart #1 Interests, Skills, Jobs

My Interests	My Skills	My Jobs
Boating	Teaching	Sailing Instructor
People	Organizing	Human Resources
Health Care	Writing	Web Writer

Roadmap Chart #2: Interests, Skills, Training

If you look ahead down the road, your combination of interests and your wish for a certain type of job, may involve gaining a few more skills, and also more formal training to learn those skills. How can you move from your "Interests," to further skills and training that lead to the job(s) you'd enjoy? Here's another Roadmap Chart to help guide you. Look especially at the fact that "time" is included in this Chart. This is important in making decisions.

Interests	Skills	Training	Time
Sailing	Navigation	Sailing School	1 yr.
	Boat Building	Apprenticeships	6 mos.
	Boat Racing	Experiential	1 yr.
Writing	Interviewing	Experiential	6 mos.
	Web Design	Web Certification	3 wks.
	News Reporting	Internship	6 mos.
Med Tech	Ultrasound	Training Program	6 mos.

You may want to ask yourself questions, to help in filling out the chart:

What do I want to do in the near future, let's say the next 3 - 6 months? Which interests of mine can turn into a job in that time period? Or do I want to look farther ahead, and take more time to develop my skills? Am I OK doing what I'm doing now for a certain period of time? How long can I 'stand it' and would I be able to wait longer to make a change? Or does it need to be very soon?

As you are looking over your Charts above, there are a few new steps that you can take, and questions to ask, that will help you even further to narrow down your decisions to your ' time zone' for planning ahead and going where you want to go. When you take a long trip, on an airplane, by train or bus, you may find that you switch time zones. What time will it be when you arrive, you wonder? If you start at noon on the East Coast on your journey, and you go to California, when do you arrive? It's important to know!

So, just as you plan ahead for any journey and you want to know your departure and arrival times, on your life journey, you'll want to know this, as well. When do I start my trip towards a new job and new skills to match my passions? When do I get there?

The next Chart, below, will help you to answer the questions that you can use to know when you'll 'arrive' at your skill and job destinations. Just as on a long journey you may take that trip in stages, perhaps first by bus, then a train, then a plane, in creating a life transition, your steps may be taken in stages, with ' rest stops' along the way. But to start out, you'll need to know how many legs there are on your journey, and what those rest stops will be, how long each part of the journey will take. This can help you to see that the journey is not nearly as tiring or as stressful as you might think it would be! Looking ahead can help! You can feel more relaxed by knowing the steps ahead and that you *will* get there!

Look back at your Charts above, and ask yourself:

*What are the steps I can take that will get me where I want to go - in stages? If I want to be a nurse, for example, can the first stop along the way be that I'll first train as a lab technician, and get a certificate to work in a lab in the next 6 months? Maybe my second stop will be that I'll then work in a lab as I am going for my L.P.N. degree. Then I'll work as an L.P.N. as I go for my R.N.

So, getting your nursing degree may be a fun process in which you don't have to wait forever to go into your field of interest, you go there on a journey in stages, and at each stage, you get to rest awhile, enjoy the new skills you've gained, and then move on when you're ready.

Knowing the steps, and how they 'combine' to make the longer trip doable, is important. You'll want to ask yourself the following question:

*How can I break this journey down into steps that I can do, one after another, in order to take myself to the next goal in my life, and not wait forever?

While you'll want to have this information, you may not know the answers yourself, immediately. Luckily, there are many trained professionals in the fields of your interest, whatever that interest may be, who can help you to know the information you need. Turn to them! Ask them for details and advice! They can help you to make the next Roadmap Chart, up ahead, so you can structure your journey for your own timeline. Ask yourself the following question:

* Whom can I contact, to get for more information about which steps I need to take? Who are the resource people to help me with the information I need to set up my timeline, and the rest stops along the way in my life journey?

Here's Roadmap Chart #3 to help with the next steps:

Roadmap Chart #3

My Skills	My Training	My Information
Med Tech	Ultrasound	3 Schools
		Speak w/Admissions
Sailing	Boat Building	Contact 3 Builders
		Ask about apprenticeships and training
Writing	Web Design	Contact Certification Programs
		Look at costs & time
		Call local library
		Free Design Courses
Nursing	Lab Tech, LPN, RN, NP	Program Catalog
		Speak w/Admissions

Deciding How to Decide

When you are in the middle of looking over your life choices, especially a career path, it's easy to feel overwhelmed. You can feel anxious when thinking about the choices. Fear can stop many people in their tracks. If you do start to feel nervous about making important decisions, what can you do? It's tempting to run from decisions, but this may not be the way to avoid the future, which will arrive whether decisions are made, or not. How can you face decisions with without anxiety about making choices?

Calm Down: And Keep Deciding!

Calm inner dialogue ' with yourself,' can be a great frame of mind, and even a new ' habit' that you can develop, when choosing among alternatives and creating a plan. Taking each choice in turn, and looking over that choice, is one way to contemplate how the future may develop. After each choice you consider, thinking about your life ahead if you made that choice, you can then choose the next option. Repeat this process through all of your choices. Imagining the future given that particular choice, will help you to see how your life can unfold differently through the choices you made.

Checking In: How Do You Feel? Emotions Count!

When you consider each choice, how do you feel about it? Does that particular life path, down the road a year, two years, five years from now - seem to you to be one that you would enjoy? Do you feel passionate about it, excited about the idea of that work, the daily life you would lead? Trying to explore 'daily life' in your choices, after you receive the skills, training, new knowledge, and design your life with your new choice in mind, does it seem to be that you'd be happy and satisfied with that choice? Putting your 'head' and also your ' heart' into your choice will help you to be committed and see it through when you are learning the skills to get you to the next day, and week, and month, and then to reach your goals.

A List of the 'Pros' and ' Cons' - Focusing!

When you have narrowed down your choice to just 2 or 3 options, it's time to look at the 'nitty gritty' and see how each choice measures up when you compare it to the others. Your list might look something like this:

Option 1: Nurse		Option 2: Medical Writer	
Work Hours		Work Hours	
Pay & Benefits		Pay & Benefits	
Interesting?		Interesting?	
Exciting?		Exciting?	

Option 1: Nurse		Option 2: Medical Writer	
Hard/Easy?		Hard/Easy?	
Help Others?		Help Others?	
Can I Grow?		Can I Grow?	
Best/Worse		Best/Worse	
A Job I Want?		A Job I Want?	
In 5 years		In 5 years	

As you learn to use your own charts, you may find you'll fill them out more than once. Indeed, you may have a stack of papers next to you on your desk, with different types of answers, timelines, interests. As Lorraine Hansberry, playwright, reminds us, taking the time to think is good! The European philosopher, Martin Heidegger, called this process "building, dwelling, and thinking." First, you can build the charts above, based upon your interests, passions, curiosities, and the concrete information about various professions, including training and timelines. Then, take time to dwell! Explore how you feel about the various alternatives. Do the 'Imaginary Road' exercises! Examine your changing feelings about the various paths you could lead. If you're feeling stuck in one pathway and not entirely comfortable with where it leads, think about your role as Construction Manager on the *Life Thruway.* The choice of road building is yours. It can take some time, but the time is well worth it to the outcome. It's your life you are choosing, the life journey ahead. It is worth the time and care you put into the design and construction of your pathway.

From Practice To Practical!

Give yourself the time to decide, and explore your life pathways and career or job choices more than once, allowing your ideas and feelings to simmer, change, develop, and then - settle into what feels best to you, considering all the options, both the intangible and the tangible issues - how you feel, how much you'll earn, where you'll go for training, the time it will take, and the various issues discussed above.

When making a big choice about choosing a new pathway in life, your emotions may go up and down during the decision-making process. You may want to fill out the table above several times, without looking at your former replies. Do this on different days. You will want to explore your ' short list' of life choices when you are in different moods, so that you can filter out the passing emotions that may have to do with a hard day, or monies worries that day, or other influences. Then, when you do make a choice, 'live with the choice,' for a week. When you wake up each day, imagine your future with the choice you have made, and see how it feels - for a full week. Are you feeling 'better' each day about the choice, or worse? Are you getting excited about your future, or are you getting cold feet? You will want to 'wear' your decision sufficiently so that you are settled on it.

Finding the Right School for the Right Training

Then, you are ready to look for a school that will provide you with the opportunity to reach your future career and life goals. That next decision is often more concrete than this one. You are almost ready for smooth sailing ahead.

Matching Your Career Choice with a School

There are many, many people who went to non-ivy league schools and are very successful in life. You do not need to go to a school that is beyond your means financially, is too far away, or is a school you choose only because it is called an ' ivy.' You can choose your school based upon its reputation, yes but also the other parameters that are important to you.   Do you want to commute from home? Are you interested in a big or small school? Does the school have courses that match your interests? Is Financial Aid available if you need it?   What about career guidance after you finish your degree or during your studies? If you have any challenges in life such as a physical disability, does the school provide easy access and support? Are there academic services such as a good library, a tutoring center, and advisors, to help you with your goals towards success academically?

What about flexibility of schedule? Can you attend at night, or just during the day? Are you able to take a part-time course load or is full-time required? Can you take some courses online if you wish, or even, your entire degree online? Do you take courses with people of similar age, or is the school diverse age-wise? If you are a parent, are there childcare facilities? What about commuting support, such as local trains or busses? What other elements would you seek in your ' ideal school' and then which schools match up to your list of 'necessities,' and your ' preferences'?

Finding the right school, just as choosing a pathway through school, take time, but the time put into these decisions is well worth it regarding your level of challenge to your time, resources, and energy, as well as your focus, once you are committed to your pathway.

If the school is too far away, you may find yourself just too tired every day to concentrate. If it is too expensive, you can run out of funds half way through your studies. If it is local, not expensive, has a great support structure, on the other hand, for an individual with a disability and offers accessibility to all services, and offers the degree choices you are interested in, perhaps it is a school that adds up to the right place for you. Making a list of school requirements, school' options,' and your ' bottom line,' will be important in choosing the right school for you.

Similarly, in job choices, today it may seem that you cannot pick and choose jobs, but often in a field that is focused and in which you have developed your skills and talents, you can find options jobwise. Your questions aside from salary might include benefits, time off for vacations, commuting, opportunities for advancement, the exact job responsibilities, and fellow co-worker environment, as well as other types of questions such as whether it is a personal environment in getting to know others, or whether it is a less personal structure and environment.

You will want to make your 'top preferences' list, and 'what you'd accept,' as well as your 'bottom line' below which you will not accept a job. It is as important to have a 'bottom line,' as it is to have a set of 'top choices.' You would not want to put an enormous amount of time and energy into choosing a career path, going to school or other types of training, only to settle for much lower on your job expectations than you originally wished for.

Make sure the house you are walking into both regarding the choices you make in school, job-wise, is one that you would want to dwell within and that you'd feel happy in, rather than 'just being barely able to stand being there.' That's not a good place to land, and you will wish you had not made that choice. Finding ways to 'hold out' for the better position that you feel you'd like, is important.

Your Guides and Mentors Can Go with You

Remembering that you have guides and mentors, and you are not alone, is important when choosing your direction in life, when going down your pathway, and also, upon arrival at your destination. You do not need to give up guides and mentors as you grow and change. Your needs for them may change, but you can always to turn to them, and ask for guidance, whether it is of a practical, a spiritual, or an emotional nature. Your decisions, when assisted by the guidance of people who have your best interests in mind, will be stronger for the advice you have sought and heard, and it will certainly help you to feel, and to be, both more independent, and also, at the same time, part of a community of people who share your sense of the importance of making good choices in life- that is, choices that are right *for you.*

Balancing Life, School, Work

Choosing a school major or course of concentrated study, doesn't mean letting go of every other interest you have in life. Many people have found that staying well-rounded is a key to feeling happy both in school, and when on the job you do after school. You may find that your interests even ' trade places' through the course of your life. The Monty Python comedian John Cleese originally went to law school at Cambridge, in England. Farther back, the writer of *Ivanhoe*, Sir Walter Scott, had studied law, too, and even became a criminal defense lawyer. He was Scottish, and his imagination roamed over the English countryside. Instead of abandoning his imagination to his work, Sir Walter Scott held his court clerk position, which gave him a decent income to live on, and simultaneously, he wrote his romance stories filled with beautiful tales and stories based upon the myths of England and Scotland.

Even in other types of fields, it may be surprising to learn that individuals who found a passion in life that they followed, did not do only that from the start of life, but indeed, had other professions, as well. The painter Henri Matisse, was such a superb artist that it is hard to imagine him doing anything other than art all day long! It was pure chance that when Matisse came down with appendicitis earlier in life, he had to spend an entire year recuperating. During that time, concerned he would be bored and needed activity that was not too physically strenuous, Matisse's mother decided that perhaps painting would be a recuperation type of distraction. We know what happened next - and Matisse's art is now in museums around the world. What were his life plans before the appendicitis? He was anticipating working as an administrator.

Today, it is difficult to think that this great artist had another goal in mind. Yet, in life the pathways that are our true passions, when we design the road there, or when, at times, by serendipity, the road opens up to us, at that point, we are on our way.

Your Life Pathway: A Source of Energy!

Perhaps most famous of all, Albert Einstein worked registering other people's patents, as a clerk in a patent office, while on the side figuring out the relationship of energy to matter, out of his passion for the subject. By burning the midnight oil pursuing his fascination with physics, after working in a clerk's day job, he managed to give to the world, his discovery immortalized in the mathematics phrase: $E = MC^2$.

Traveling Two Roads at One Time!

In the examples above, the individuals mentioned were about to embark upon one path, but another showed up, and they followed their passions. At times, there was overlap or a second profession was chosen, and followed, for a long while. Einstein's years as a patent clerk were not many, but it was suited to his nighttime labors figuring out physics issues, to have his day job.

Indeed, there are many people today who actually do hold two or more types of jobs at the same time. It may be economic necessity, or it may be by choice. The U.S. Labor Department statistics indicate that at least seven million people, and likely more, have more than one job at a time. It may be a day job and a night job, or jobs that take place at different times of the year, or jobs at a workplace and at home. One job may be a ' creative job,' the other job, perhaps more practical in nature. The choice on job combinations is yours to make, and often the two jobs can balance one another out very comfortably, both regarding interests, and also, extra income.

Your Own Unique Road Ahead

As you've been exploring your life passions and skills, assessing the balance of your talents and the careers that might match these, and looking at the ways to overcome obstacles in traveling on your pathway, perhaps the question of 'why' is becoming clearer to you. You may be feeling that you want to make changes in your life, and that you are gaining faith in the idea that the future can be more fulfilling than you'd imagined it could be. Any time a new road is taken, there are choices in which other roads are not taken. It takes courage to make a choice, and to begin to travel down your unique road in life. Your journey ahead, while you can plan it from every angle, will have surprises. The unexpected cannot be planned - for in specific detail. Yet your attitude, your approach, your sense of courage and commitment, may make the difference between running away, stopping in your tracks, making big detours, or not completing the road you have chosen to travel. It is decidedly a courageous act to choose a new direction in life.

> *"Do not be too timid or squeamish...All life is an experiment. The more experiments you make, the better."*
>
> *- Ralph Waldo Emerson*

> *"Courage is rarely reckless or foolish...courage usually involves a highly realistic estimate of the odds that must be faced."*
>
> *- Margaret Truman*

If you are a religious person, you may find that turning to guidance and faith can help you in sustaining courage, as you walk down your path in life, forging your future with faith and hope. In the Proverbs, following one's heart is a form of faith that is powerful, and rings true in all eras of humanity, from thousands of years ago, to your time, today. *"More than all else, keep watch over your heart, since here are the wellsprings of life." - Proverbs 4:23*

Chapter Five

Stumbling Blocks! Everyone Has Them!

Boulders vs. Stumbling Blocks

You may know of the Greek story of Sisyphus, who pushed a boulder up a hill, and then had to push it up a hill - again, and again. What a thankless task! The boulder was heavy, and Sisyphus kept on doing the same thing - pushing the same boulder, of the same size, up the same hill. No wonder Sisyphus is the tale of the individual who has an inevitable task ahead of him, that does not get easier - ever. And it is partly of his own making that he is stuck with the boulder, every single day.

What happens when you try to push a big boulder uphill for more than 5 minutes? You run out of energy and start to feel exhausted! After 10 minutes? You're thinking 'uh -oh' I could get flattened by this boulder! After 15 minutes? You hear a scraping noise. The boulder is stopping. It's moving backwards. Duck!

Run! Dash back to the bottom of the hill! Get outta there! The boulder goes crashing by, and you barely escape being crushed.

That's when life feels a burden - a big boulder about to push you aside. When you know you're up against a boulder - a seemingly impossible, insurmountable life situation, then often the best thing to do is find a way to get out of the situation, and not get crushed by it.

Yet, fortunately, no one has to be Sisyphus, since as mere mortals, we are able to make decisions and choose to follow pathways that are, at least in part, of our own design. Choosing which road to follow, which hills and valleys to travel, you can look at the obstacles you encounter, and you can decide how these obstacles will be dealt with. You do not have to roll the boulder of Sisyphus up the same hill, and carry a burden each day of an obstacle that may show up. You can choose what to do with that obstacle, and choose your way around it. The boulder does not even have to remain a boulder. You can change it into something more manageable. And, indeed, first things first. Is it actually a big boulder you are encountering? Or something smaller, easier, and certainly not an obstacle that would stop you in your tracks. An obstacle does not have to become the boulder of Sisyphus in your life. What will you do to change that scenario?

When you are on your way towards your goals, and you are encountering obstacles here and there, don't mistake molehills for mountains. Ask yourself, "*Is this really a giant boulder that is going to flatten me? Or is it more of a stumbling block?"* Learning to see what is an insurmountable obstacle, and look at the difference between that and a stumbling block, is an important aspect of finding your way towards your goals. Even when obstacles show up, there is often a way around them, over or under, or by taking a slightly different route that will still get you where you are going.

Pam, a home health aide working at $10 an hour, with no benefits, and little time off, faced a question about different routes to solve a problem, literally! She had enrolled in night school to meet the requirements and take courses so she could get into a program to become a dental hygienist. All was going well and she was able to get from her job to school by taking a bus directly from her last client of the day, that landed her right in front of the community college where she was studying at night. Then, everything changed when Pan was assigned a different client for the end of the day. The new client was in a neighborhood with no bus route. Mid-terms were coming up, she had to make sure not to miss any classes. This felt like a mountain. Flunking out of school the first term was not in Pam's goal for life. She decided that rather than letting this be a boulder that would push her over, she'd find another route, around it.

At school, Pam looked for a bulletin board for student notices. She put up a big sign in bold letters "Ride share needed right away, please call! Happy to help with gas!" Within 24 hours, another student had called, who could pick her up from her last job, and ride share with Pam to school. The mountain had turned into a molehill. A stumbling block had been resolved.

Not every stumbling block gets solved easily. It may take time, and creative thinking, to figure out the solution. Taking a good look at the situation and deciding, *"Is this a boulder, is it a stumbling block?"* will help. If you think you're facing a boulder, you can look at it from a few different angles. Is there a way to break it down into smaller pieces? What might make this a few smaller stumbling blocks instead of what seems like one big impossible-to-get-around obstacle?

Think of the guys who work in road construction, when they have a road to repair. Faced with solid blocks of concrete, this may appear to be an impossible job. How will tons of pavement be moved and cleared away, to fix the problem? One solution works! Break it down to smaller pieces. Then that very same huge obstacle suddenly becomes possible to move.

Dealing with a problem often means finding out what works to transform it into smaller parts. Then, the mountain, the boulder, the road, the obstacle- can be removed.

In Josh's case, he was faced with a big obstacle, and one he never saw, until it hit him. Josh was in school working on his electrician's license. He'd enrolled in the National Guard, a few years back, and was on reserve duty. He figured he'd get through school and just make time for the weekend reserve trainings, without a conflict between the reservist duties and his school work. All went well for 8 months. Then, Josh was called up and found himself overseas helping with a military supply unit far from home. It seemed a safe enough place to be deployed. He wasn't on the front lines. Then a roadside bomb nobody had anticipated, hit his supply truck. Josh underwent surgery, and came home missing his right leg from the knee down.

It was a number of months before he felt that he could face the future. Josh looked within, and found that he had not given up on his goals. It was going to be a road filled with obstacles that he hadn't seen before. But he decided he had to move ahead. He had seen buddies in worse shape, who had pulled through. Josh wasn't going to quit. But he didn't know how to succeed, either. The biggest issue for Josh was not that his dreams had disappeared, but that he just didn't know how in the world he'd get there. He had learned how to walk with a prosthetic calf and foot, and was regaining his strength. Yet the very idea of getting to and from school seemed insurmountable. He couldn't drive. He didn't have money to hire anybody to help him. He didn't live close enough to school to walk. How was he going to be able to finish his studies? And then, even if he could graduate, how would he have the mobility to get around, and serve his customers, once he got his electrician's license?

Everything loomed large. There appeared to be not just one, but a number of boulders, teetering on a ledge above him. Josh saw the boulders in anxious nightmares at night. He felt like his life was about to cave in. He asked himself, if there were alternatives to letting them crash down. What was the way to clear out the path ahead?

One thing Josh knew, he couldn't solve these problems, of this magnitude, on his own. He decided to take a very clear snapshot of the boulders up on the ledge, and lay out the picture of his situation to others, who had the experience to help him out.

Chapter Six

Mentors & Guides: Everyone Needs Them!

As you explore farther within your life choices, whether you are making a momentous decision to finish a college degree or change your career – more opportunities, and also a specific set of 'routes' to follow will open up to you. Once you have made the first decision, others come into the picture. How do you decide, not knowing exactly what is ahead, and how it will feel once you get there? A lot is at stake. Should you become a nurse, or go for all the years it takes to be a doctor? Which would you like better? Should you take your certification in web design, or go for the State teaching certification to teach technology in school? Should you finish up your A.A. first, or go right into the more arduous B.A. program? Is it better to have a major in history, which you love, or a major in accounting, which is also interesting? Which direction will you like better? You've written down all the ' plusses' and ' minuses' on a sheet of paper. You've looked at job statistics giving salaries, and future growth in your interest area, job-wise. You've read up on the requirements for the jobs. But how do you know what's right for you? A crystal ball would be great right about now. You could peer into it, see yourself in 3 years, 5 years, 10 years, and discover which choice is going to be best for you. But though you try to 'imagine,' it is all theoretical, on paper. It would be great if somebody could help you to decide.

Important but also often more complicated than you anticipated, the follow-up decisions after you've chosen a larger direction, can catch you unawares. 'I'm finishing my degree. I want my B.A. OK! All set! I've decided what I'm going to do!' The application is submitted. The course catalog arrives. You open it, and realize you can choose among 35 majors, and 20 minors. You have required courses, electives, and then, even courses you can design for yourself, as Independent Study. You are trying to make decisions, not just what to register for next term, but- the big picture. How can you see into the future and know what will work best for you?

Imaginary Exercise: The House of Your Dreams

Imagine you are about to step into a house. You have longed to visit this house, it has caught your eye every time you have passed by and seen it. The house may be the house of your dreams!

Yet, in order to go inside you are told that have to make a few commitments in advance. Going inside the house and all of its beautiful interior, as well as the back yard, the pool and the beautiful gardens, first requires that you decided to sign on the dotted line. You're not buying the house to live in it forever. But you want to go in and look around. You have a feeling it might be the house of your dreams. However, first to look around, you have to commit, on paper, to register for the courses you'll take for 4 years in your college program.

You have to choose which courses. Certain choices you are free to make, will help you to walk in the door of this lovely home. Other choices take you to the house down the street, the house around the corner, the house in a different neighborhood. All of these other houses may be great, once you get to know the neighborhood better. But you are pretty sure you want to live in *this* house. Walking in the door will take you 4 years. You have to choose before you walk in the door, what you'll do, in detail, those 4 years up ahead. It feels like a big set of decisions, just to go inside and see this lovely house!

Standing on the curb, you look at the house longingly. There are wonderful decorations outside, flowers, a lamp post, a walkway lined with mosaics. The house beckons to you. But what if you do 4 years of hard work, step inside, and it's the wrong house for you?

So, as your hand is on the door handle, you turn and ask the first person you see walking by, ' *What will I find inside this house?'* *Can you tell me, I want to know in advance, before I go inside!'*

The first person you happen to see answers, '*I've never been on this block, I am just passing through. I have no idea what the interior of this house is like, let alone any of the houses nearby.*'

The second person stops, thinks a moment or two, and says '*I know the neighborhood around the corner. It is a great place to be. But I can't tell you what you'll find inside, before you open the door to this house. I see you're eager to go in, but you want more information. I can't help. someone who has visited here or even lived here, can probably help you.*'

Then you see a third person. She is walking in a relaxed manner, confident and comfortable. She is holding a few groceries, and humming a tune. '*Do you know this house?*' you ask. '*Could you tell me what it's like inside? I may even want to live here, but I have to commit to my college courses, for 4 years it's a lot of commitment, to walk into this house.*' '*I want to have an idea before I walk inside if it's for me.*'

The woman looks at you and smiles. '*As a matter of fact, 6 years ago I was in the same predicament. Indeed, that was the very house I looked at. I wanted to know what was inside, just as you do. I noticed that the door was unlocked. I could have turned the handle. But still, I was afraid about those 4 years, too.*' *So, as you are doing now, I asked for advice. And I am happy now to help you, and tell you how it was for me to walk into that house, and to live there. I had many wonderful experiences. There were challenging times. But I learned, I grew, I was happy. What specifically are your questions? Let me see how I can help you to see if this house is right for you!'*

The house, as you know, is a metaphor. It is a symbol. It can represent the place where you want to be in the future. The house is your job - the job as a translator that you yearn to get. The house is your first business you'll found and create.

Wanting to step inside, to see what will be there, and how you will feel 'living' inside the profession you choose- is a natural wish. Everybody would love to be assured, and to have the question answered, *'When I turn the door handle, and step inside, after long preparations for to enter and dwell within the dream job I've trained for, will I like being there? What will I find?'*

A particular characteristic of doors that lead to new places, is that as you open them, and step across the threshold, you can only glimpse a partial view of what's ahead, before you step inside that dwelling place of the future. Turning that door handle, and opening the door, is an act of courage, and of faith in the future. *'Of course,'* you muse to yourself, *'concrete information will help!'* *'I know how I feel when I walk in, will be unique to me. Yet a little information in advance can help!'*

Guides and Mentors: You'll Find Them!

Asking for advance guidance from people who know the landscape, the territory, the neighborhood, is often very helpful.

And especially, sitting with people who know the particular house on the block, and have been inside, can be quite reassuring.

These individuals may become your guides and mentors. Finding them may be as random as asking strangers on a street, but more likely, you can discover guides and mentors by thinking ahead, and looking around. If you want to become a furniture designer, then it can be enormously helpful to look not only to speak with an experienced furniture designer, but also, a designer whose work you admire, or whose career trajectory is inspiring to you. Discovering the individuals who may become guides or mentors does not need to be an arduous task. You may find people whose work is of interest to you, by turning to resources in the field. Is there a website devoted to fine furniture making today? Are there interviews in a trade magazine, with interesting furniture makers? Is there a furniture making shop in your community? What about the workshop given once a month locally on making wooden cabinets, at the furniture outlet?

Look around. Make a list with names and phone numbers, of people who are in the field you'd you would like to enter. Call. Set up an appointment. Indicate you want to ask a few questions as you are thinking of training for the profession. Often people will be very generous with their time and advice.

From a short-term guide, an individual who may meet with you once or twice, to finding a long-term mentor, may be another step in your quest to explore your path ahead. Whether the 'mentor' knows everything about the field you will enter, or not, what is important is that this individual has a sense of *you* and can listen to *your* questions and dilemmas, and help you to find your way.

A guide who knows the field can help with concrete steps. A mentor may have a sense of how *you* would feel given the atmosphere ahead. Mentor relationships are to be cherished and may develop quickly, or, over time. Perhaps you may already know a person, even an individual you have known for many years, who is someone you admire. You may feel this person has wisdom, and can offer guidance to you at a level in which he or she knows not only the decisions you need to make, but also has a sense of you, as a person, and what would be best for you, from *your* perspective.

A guide may be the expert who can help you by saying 'To become the owner of a small business, you'll need these four courses, they will really help you with your organizational skills.' A mentor may say, 'You are pushing yourself with being a perfectionist! You're giving yourself too much stress! Let's talk about a different way to think about success! What does it mean to you?'

Everybody needs both guides, and mentors. While self-guidance and self-mentoring are wonderful to do, there is often much to be gained by turning to others with experience that you think is valuable to have in life. This may be professional work experience, or intrinsic intuition and wisdom. There are often both intangible and tangible factors that go into finding the right guides and mentors. Looking for practical, real-life experience in that individual, which parallels what you are seeking in your life, is a great starting point.

A mentor may be a friend, a relative, a teacher, in the clergy, a Rabbi, or a person you met across a crowded room, with whom you found a strong connection as fellow human beings. It may be surprising that our mentors are not necessarily years older than we are, but perhaps they *do*turn out to be our elders. Have you ever chatted with a person who is younger than you are, and found that this individual was ' older than his years' in soul-wisdom?   The intuition you may have, ' This person is offering me guidance, let me stop and listen carefully,' can only come from you. But you'll know it when you encounter a guide or a mentor. This person will help you, and not seek to hinder your forward progress with your life path. He or she will not jump in and act competitively towards you, wanting what you have or feeling jealous. He or she will not say ' Do exactly as I did, and you'll be an instant success.' Instead, the individual who is a true guide and mentor will often ask you questions, listen with an open heart and mind, offer words of advice but not mandates, and will express support, clearly wanting the best for you.

You may hear words of advice that you may disagree with, or agree with. You may choose a direction a little different from that which your mentors or guides may gently encourage you towards. In fact, you may choose a totally different route, all your own, after consulting with a mentor or a guide. What is important is that the individual will not harshly judge you, or ask you to make yourself exactly into his or her copy, or require forms of acquiescence or servitude from you.

Mentors and guides may have their own highly positive sense of self, and personal direction. Yet they will not demand that you precisely follow in their tracks. Open dialogue in which you feel you are able to make important choices, with support, will be the hallmark of good mentoring guidance. Don't settle for someone who says ' be just like me.' Ego can speak loudly, but is not always speaking from the right place. A true mentor or guide will realize that your decisions will be yours to make, in becoming uniquely you.

The Imaginary House Exercise Revisited

The woman on the street who stopped and smiled when you asked her '*Will I like it inside this house I'm about to work 4 years to enter?*' - looks at the house and says, '*Well, it may be different for you, but for me... this is what I loved, and this is what happened there. I will offer you my story, but mostly, I'd like to hear yours. Then I can have a sense if you'll like this house, when you go inside.*'

Chapter Seven

Befriending The Journey

—॥॥—

"I wish to live because life has within it that which is good, that which is beautiful and that which is love. Therefore, since I have known all of these things, I have found them to be reason enough and—I wish to live.

Moreover, because this is so, I wish others to live for generations and generations and generations."

- Lorraine Hansberry "A Raisin in the Sun"

The American playwright, Lorraine Hansberry, faced many obstacles in reaching for her dream to become a writer. As a female, as an African-American individual, writing plays for the stage, it was nearly impossible for Lorraine to be taken seriously as a person pursuing her passionate work in life. Ms. Hansberry drew inspiration from goodness, from beauty, from love. Seeing life as a gift to be grateful for, and to celebrate, she asked what it feels like to go beyond living day-to-day without direction, or subject to other people's ideas about who you are, and what you should be doing.

Asking "What do I love, what direction should I take in life?" takes courage. Answering that question takes even more courage! You may be concerned, "The obstacles I may face - will I learn how to overcome them?" After all the thought, discussion, research, and planning is done, starting the journey does not require that you show up with every solution to every potential problem, ready-made. It is unlikely most people would set foot outside the front door and into the world, if all problems had to have guaranteed solutions, in advance. A set of guides, a good sense of direction, tools and skills, these are all very helpful. It's certainly true that you've got a better chance at success on your journey if you have paid attention to your packing list.

Every person who has tried to move from "here" to "there" has had to do exactly the same thing to get "there" and that is: take the first step. Whether that step is picking up the phone and asking a potential mentor or guide to meet with you, or making a list of your skills, or registering for a course, each step takes you to the next step.

Imaginary Exercise: A Very Long Road

Imagine for a moment that you are about to sign up to travel from start to finish on a road that is very long. In fact, this road, even if you were to travel around the Earth several times, would be farther than those tens of thousands of miles. The path you are traveling is 238,857 miles long- rather long, indeed. You don't have time for too much pondering about whether you could have taken a different road, and you can't turn around until you reach your destination.

Once you've signed up, you're committed to this particular trip. No rest stops, no detours! After 3 days, 3 hours, and 39 minutes- to be exact- you arrive. You may be feeling "there's no place like home" and thinking "I'll just do a quick U-turn back to familiar territory, yet..." you've traveled a very long way just to take a quick look and not even explore your surroundings. Instead of peeking out the window of your vehicle, you decide to be bold. "OK, I've come this far, let me take one more step," you decide.

In July of 1969 a man made just that choice.

"That's one small step for Man, one giant leap for Mankind," said Astronaut Neil Armstrong, as he hopped off the final rung of the ladder of a small lunar module, and became the first human being ever to set foot on the Moon.

And what a journey it was! Even though the tools were just newly developed, the packing was rudimentary, and not everything had already stood the test of time, the destination lay ahead. The best way to go - and return! - to this new destination had not yet even been established. What a way to start a trip - hurtling through time and space to a destination never seen up close and in person!

The Astronauts climbed on board. They had mentors and guides far away, helping, but their courage had to be right there, with them, in the module. When you put on that seat belt you definitely hope it will work. And then, you adjust your sights for the road ahead. Looking in the rearview mirror will only get you so far. Oops! There goes the Earth! The tether is no longer attached! You will need to actually look ahead, and envisage your trip, as well as your destination. It may be dark outside, but inside, you have provisions. You have light. You have guidance systems. You know - approximately- where you are headed!

Upon his return from the Moon, Neil Armstrong described the calculation tools in the lunar module, that he and his crew used to help determine how to get to the Moon - and back. He said, "the power available to the Apollo Landing module was less than what you now have in your scientific calculator." Compared even to today's smart phones, Armstrong has said, the Apollo's tools to calculate the exact journey would be "put to shame." The journey to the Moon had been dreamt of for thousands of years. The tools were not perfect, but they were good enough to go ahead. The preparations included support of guides, a road map that was well-thought-out, and a step-by-step itinerary with an estimated arrival time. As much as could be reasonably planned ahead of time, helped Armstrong to take that step, from the known, to the unknown.

To the Moon? You've Got to be Kidding!

"A Moon landing? You'd have to be 100% sure everything would work to perfection trying!" you may be thinking to yourself. "What if I don't have everything perfectly in order? What if there are no guarantees?"

You might think that the Moon Astronauts had every detail perfectly worked out as 100% fail-safe. How did Armstrong actually feel? After landing on the Moon, he said, "I was elated, ecstatic, and extremely surprised that we were successful. "

You may be feeling, "Would I want to try something in my life that feels as scary as going to the Moon?" Guess what? Neil Armstrong was not sure of his outcome of his trip. But he added up all the important tools, put them in his backpack, looked behind, looked ahead- and then - he blasted off!

What did the Astronauts who went to the Moon hope to do? They didn't want to hang out on the back lawn home again. Well-maybe for awhile! Rest and rejuvenation are definitely required before and after challenging journeys! But then -they wanted to go to Mars, afterwards! The Moon was challenging. But what about Mars? Or other places in the Universe? What they found was that there was a lot to learn right there, on the Moon. Many people decided that the journey was far enough, while others had a different goal in mind.

Your 'Moon' might be reaching that destination of walking down the aisle with a cap and gown, to the graduation stage to be handed your new diploma. Perhaps it is your EMS certification, and being in the ambulance driver's seat. Or maybe your goal is, "First the Moon, then Mars!"

Speaking about the importance of making choices in life, the Astronaut Neil Armstrong also said, "I believe that every human being has a finite number of heartbeats and I don't intend to waste any of mine."

As you make your choices in life' s turning points, and follow your new direction, your heart may be thumping with excitement, and perhaps trepidation, too. One thing is sure: as you find your pathway and take off into your personal future, the road ahead will be filled with new discoveries, and it will be like no other road. It will be a road dreamed, and designed, and traveled, by you.

You are here in life as uniquely you. The more you discover, as Mark Twain said, the why of living, and apply your passions and skills to this 'why, the more you will feel fulfilled in your particular purpose on Earth, for which you've been given an extraordinary gift, that of being alive.

~~END~~

About The Authors

Dr. Horace Batson, received his Ph.D. in Clinical Psychology from the Graduate School and University Center in 1980. He also received his Masters of Philosophy (M.Phil.) degree from the same institution in 1980. He co-founded Kensington Health, a national healthcare company in 1996 specializing in hiring nurse practitioners and psychologists who provided medical counseling to renal patients in dialysis facilities throughout the U.S. Dr. Batson has served as President of Welstar Publications, a publishing company dedicated to developing and promoting motivational, autobiographical and how-to-books for non-profit CEOs and entertainers. He has published over 50 books.

He has consulted to companies such as Bell Labs, The Chase Manhattan bank, hospitals, and the New York Select Committee on Child Abuse. Dr. Batson served as smoking cessation psychologist for The American Health Foundation's Multiple

Risk Factor Intervention Trial (MRFIT), was the project director for Cornell Medical College's Laboratory of Health Behavior Research smoking prevention study and Project Director for the Addiction Research and Treatment Corporation's (ARTC), Treatment Research Unit (TRU) funded by the National Institute on Drug Abuse. Dr. Batson consults to both nonprofit and for profit companies since 1984. He specializes in behavior management for special needs individuals with self-injurious, disruptive and violent behavior. Currently, Dr. Horace Batson is a senior partner with Batson Communications. Dr. Batson serves as adjunct professor of psychology at many New York private and CUNY colleges. He has published in peer reviewed journals.

Dr. Gary Batson, is President of Batson Communications & Entertainment Company. He earned his BA from Fordham University, his MA from Columbia University with a specialization in Communications, and his D.M. (Doctor of Management) from the University of Maryland. His clients have included: IBM, AT&T Information System, Channel 13, and other non-profit organizations. He is a member of the Dramatist Guild, The American Society of Composers, Authors & Publishers, The Public Relations Society of America, The Yonkers Chambers of Commerce and the United Nations Association. He is a full time professor in the Department of Language and Literature at Touro College in New York and served as adjunct professor in the English Department in the Borough of Manhattan Community College (BMCC). Gary is Executive Producer of

Phoenix Arts Inc., (formerly Mount Vernon Theatre Company a non-profit performing arts company. Gary Batson has written and produced for the stage at the Negro Ensemble Company, Frederick Douglas Creative Arts Center/Bud Schulberg Watts writers Workshop/La MaMas, Dramatic Risk, Strawberry One Act Festival and Samuel French One Act Festival...He is presently writer in residence at WCT collaborative theater (Westchester Collaborative Theater). His plays include Point of View, Richard, Ill Winds, FIRE, CODES and Olive Branch.

PART II

Implementation of Principles

Attention:
This section should be used as a Workbook
to give you practical steps to follow to achieve your goals.

1. What is (are) your passion(s)?

_____

_____

_____

_____

2.   What do you do best? What are you good at?

_____

_____

_____

_____

3.   What gets your adrenaline pumping?

_____

_____

_____

_____

4. What book or stories interest you the most?

_____

_____

_____

_____

5. When you think about yourself in the future what are you doing to make money?

_____

_____

_____

_____

6. Do the research about those things that interest you.

_____

_____

_____

7. Test out your new profession in small steps. Take baby steps. For example, if you want to be a clinical psychologist talk to your friends about their problems. Are you helpful? If not, why not?

_____

_____

_____

_____

_____

8. If you want to be a cook, try out new recipes. Have your friends taste your creation? Do they like it? If not, why not?

_____

_____

_____

_____

_____

9. Schedule enough time to adequately test out your new career.

_____

_____

_____

_____

10. Find out the various ways that you can make money and make a living doing what you want. This doesn't happen overnight, do not become discouraged. Things take time.

_____

_____

_____

_____

_____

_____

_____

11. List All of Your Skills/Abilities (e.g., computer, sales, speaking, persuasion, writing, etc.)

_____

_____

_____

_____

_____

Choosing Your Major

Now that you have determined your passion, in the real world how much money can you realistically make with your passion?

- Talk with people in the field doing what you want to do. Find out the income potential.
- Which schools teach this?
- Where are they located?
- What is the cost?
- How can you pay for it? Are there any scholarships?

What are the possible applications of your degree and possible places that you could work with your degree or its derivatives?

For example, if you majored in English where could you work outside of schools? Answer – Anywhere or any job where English is spoken.

For the list of majors below indicate where you could work (how you can make money) outside of the specific field!

- Psychology
- English
- Mathematics
- Chemistry
- Physics
- Business
- Art
- Spanish
- French
- Music

Finding The Right School

1. Review the reason(s) that you want to go to college.
2. Remember you do not have to go an ivy-league or name brand college. That is no guarantee of success.
3. Don't be in a rush to pick a major before you pick a college.
4. Finding a college that fits your personality or lifestyle is most important.

5. Start Looking for Graduate Schools At Least 1-2 Years Before You Are Ready.

6. Find out who is in charge of the program that interests you. Learn their research. Call them and make a meeting to discuss how their research interests you. Have questions prepared to ask them. This will make you sound genuinely interested in what they do. People like that.

How to Choose a Role Model

- Choose a role model you know to help you become the best version of yourself.
- Identify your bad habits, or negative aspects of your personality.
- Make a list of the key characteristics that you want to achieve.
- Build your confidence.
- Identify people who exhibit the same qualities that you wish to achieve.
- Consider someone who has a sense of purpose.
- Choose someone who makes you feel good about being you.
- Consider someone who interacts well with others
- Consider people who are top performers.
- Choose someone who is different from you.
- Learn about their successes and failures
- Choose someone that you know and observe succeeding in life in a way that resonates with your moral values and beliefs for your role model

- Do not copy your role model completely
- Develop your own style
- Remember that only deities are perfect.

The Importance of Exercise and A Proper Diet

What are the best tools for weight loss? Diet and physical activity. The key to losing weight successfully is a wholesome diet and keeping physically fit. Don't let the words put you off. A wholesome diet simply consists of eating healthier meals and watching your caloric intake. Physical fitness is just increasing your activity levels in the right ways. People often focus heavily on their eating habits when attempting weight loss, but physical activity also plays an important part. The more active you are, the more energy your body burns in the form of calories, which also contributes to weight loss.

Normal, day-to-day physical activity consists of things such as running errands, walking, gardening and cleaning. Exercise is a more formally structured type of activity that you do repetitively and with regularity. Regardless of what activities you decide on, focus on making them a regular part of your daily life. Try for about two hours of mild activity or an hour of more intense activity, such as aerobics, in the course of your week. Remember that these are just guidelines, and that you may need more activity for successful weight loss.

Diet Plans

If your goal is losing weight, there are plenty of diet plans available. All you need to do is check out popular "health" magazines. But how do you know if a given diet plan is the one for you? These are the questions you should be asking yourself:

- Are foods from all the major food groups: fruits, vegetables, grains, low-fat dairy products, lean protein sources and nuts represented?
- Are the foods included in the diet the foods you like and that you enjoy eating? Can you maintain the diet eating these foods?
- Are these foods easily found?
- Is the diet affordable?
- Is the diet nutritionally and calorically sound?
- Is exercise part of the plan?

The answers to all these questions should be yes.

The Basics of Weight Loss

Calories are the most important part of the weight loss equation. Fad diets may promise that what is important is counting carbs or eating special foods. But calories are what counts when it comes to losing weight. Weight loss occurs when you burn more calories than you take in. This can be accomplished by cutting extra calories, and from increasing the calories that you burn through physical activity. Once you have that understanding, you're ready to set your goals for weight loss and develop a plan for reaching them. You don't have to do it by yourself. Talk to your family, friends and doctor. Make sure that now is the right time and that you're ready to make some changes. Plan smart: Try to anticipate how you'll handle situations that challenge your resolve and the occasional setbacks you will encounter. If your weight is causing you health problems, you may wish to discuss weight loss surgery or medications with your doctor. If you make this choice, you will need to thoroughly discuss the benefits and the possible risks with your doctor. The key to losing weight successfully is making a commitment to changing your diet and exercise habits.

The Importance of Etiquette

If you have reached adulthood but you feel as though your manners haven't also matured, learning how to be charming might help you reach your potential. This skill set can help you to become more successful and get higher paying jobs. People learn to excel at public speaking, social skills and interview skills, as well as dining etiquette.

Social Skills

Social skills are essential to success, particularly in the workplace. In theory, the skills required for successful social interaction should be acquired easily by most people, but this is not always true. If you want, for instance, that promotion you have coveted but are lacking in a particular area, learning elements of charm and better manners might push you ahead of your competitors.

Guide for Dinner Interviews/Meetings

One of the many benefits of a successful career is going to dinner parties. These parties are not just about intelligent and witty conversation; you will also need to know how to use dinner utensils correctly. These dining skills should help you master simple dining tips such as handling your utensils, party etiquette tips on the polite way to begin and end a conversation and how to make a great impression.

Self-Improvement
Guide for Young Ladies

Young ladies who manage to present themselves with confidence and poise will be seen positively, not only by themselves, but by others. Women should learn techniques to help with:

- Creating Positive First Impressions; Presenting a Good Image
- Greetings and Introductions
- Importance of Positive Body Language
- Proper Posture and Carriage

- How to Walk, Sit and Stand Properly
- The Proper Way to Make an Entrance
- The Importance of a Pleasant Voice
- Good Conversation and Communication
- Etiquette in the Technological Age
- Personal Grooming, Style and Appropriate Dress
- Respect and Courtesy
- Everyday Civility
- Good Table Manners

Common Beauty Mistakes And How To Avoid Them

When it comes to your beauty routine, it's best to recognize your makeup wrongs and fix them. Here are the do's and the don'ts.

1. Not washing makeup brushes. To prevent the collection of dirt, oil and general gunk that can accumulate on your brushes, give them a weekly washing with a gentle cleansing soap or dishwashing soap. It only takes a few minutes and this simple task can prevent infections and other beauty troubles.

2. Your concealer is too light. Concealer should be as close to your natural skin tone as possible in order to blend properly. Using one that's too light will actually draw more attention to any issues you're trying to cover up!

3. Your foundation doesn't match your skin tone. Foundation is meant to blend in with your complexion

for natural coverage. It is not meant to be a substitute for a bronzer! Have an expert at the makeup counter perform a "color match" to find the perfect shade for you.

4. Don't curl your lashes after applying mascara. If you want your lashes to be clump-free, curling should be done before applying mascara. Curling afterwards will cause them to stick, clump and break.

5. Making too many different statements at once with your makeup. Wearing heavy makeup on your eyelids AND heavy lipstick as well? Too much. Less really is more when it comes to beauty.

Are You Dressed for Success?

The corporate boardroom was once the domain of men. Women were there, but they often hid behind conservative suits and sensible shoes. Many preferred to have their clothes and personal style go unnoticed as they began to excel in the executive arena. But the past few decades have revealed a new world, one in which value is placed on femininity. When first impressions are often built on appearance, the challenge of self-promotion for a female in today's corporate world can sometimes seem daunting. But one general theme has not changed. A man has a uniform in the business world; he knows what he is going to wear. A woman has a wider array of clothing choices, so there is more of a chance that she won't be able to capitalize upon her image. Too many style mistakes can demolish the credibility of a woman's image. For executive women, dressing for work and networking can mean having a variety of outfits ready to wear at a moment's notice. Projecting a corporate image while retaining your femininity is very important. Many times people don't realize how important first impressions are.

Women can show their feminine side through subtle details without being overly frilly. Simple things, like use of color, dress length, heels and wearing flattering clothes, really transform one's look and wardrobe. Stiletto shoes, low-cut tops and skirts that are too short appear far too often in a corporate setting. Women who appear too trendy can end up diverting the focus away from their professional skills. Fashion for the woman in today's business world is not only about wearing the right clothes or a great hairstyle. Like men, women must be aware of things like speech, word choice, body language and presentation to project themselves professionally. Hair and nails are no substitutes for a good handshake and a professional demeanor. Incorporating good fashion choices into one's overall business style can take a lot of work.

How to Behave Like a Gentleman

Men should learn

1. Basic Etiquette

2. Written and Verbal Communications

3. How to Speak Like a Gentleman

4. How to Behave Properly as a Host or a Guest at Social

Functions

5. How to Behave with a Lady

6. Proper Dating Etiquette

7. Good Grooming

8. Dressing Appropriately

9. Social Events

10. Introductions

11. How to Behave at the Dining Table

How to Manage Your Stress

Stress management starts with identifying the sources of stress in your life. They may not be immediately obvious, so make sure that you are not overlooking behavior and emotions that may increase your stress levels. It may not be that deadline that is stressing you out; it might just be your procrastination over it. Examine your attitudes and habits as closely as possible. Pay attention to excuses that you may be making, or things or people that you might be blaming it on. Keep a journal. Write down what you think caused your stress, what your feelings were about it, and how you reacted to it. Think about your coping strategies; are they healthy, or do you drink too much, smoke, use drugs or take your stress and anger out on others? Find healthier ways to cope. Do your best to adapt to stress, rather than running from it, or attempting to change something you have no control over. No one method is effective for everybody; work on discovering what calms you down, or makes you feel in control. Don't forget to ensure that you get enough sleep. Don't forget to maintain a positive outlook, it can sound corny, but it can really help you combat the stressful situations that will inevitable arise in your day-to-day life. Learn how to say "no" to people. Control your environment to as great a degree as you can. Don't hang around with people who cause you stress. Make your task list a more manageable one. Are you a perfectionist? Maybe you need to loosen up a little. Always set aside some time to relax and have fun. Watch TV, read a book, play guitar, or whatever it is that you think is fun. Alter your situation as much as you realistically can, but if you are unable to change the situation, change your reaction to it. Keep in mind that a certain amount of stress is unavoidable, and find it within yourself to accept the things that you can't change. Replace those things you can't control with things that you can control. And last, but not least, make your lifestyle a healthy one. Avoid smoking and other unhealthy habits. Eat a healthy diet, and follow a regular exercise program. You will be amazed at how much of a stress reducer this can be.

Overcoming Your Fears

Very few things can provide the "rush" that a little terror provides—so why not harness your fears in order to make your life richer? Fear is a horrible feeling; one we generally try to avoid. We are fortunate to live in a world where we can often elude such things as violence, disease and natural disasters. Instead, we watch television shows and movies, often about those very things that frighten us the most. Many times, we find ourselves attracted to fear. We frequently pay attention to accidents, or guns. There is an evolutionary advantage to this—we seem to be hardwired to keep things that are scary in front of us, for protection. One way to deal with the fear in your life is to confront it. It can help you deal with fear in a positive manner, and it will add some excitement to your life. Think about something that frightens you. Maybe you have a fear of flying. Think about your fear, and think about what keeps you from overcoming it. Quite often, this is all it takes to overcome your fear. I am not suggesting that you seek out toxic or dangerous behavior, like drug use. Think about whether the desire/fear you have expressed is destructive. If it is, come up with a different fear to confront. Try to think of something that can affect the world in a positive way; taking medicine to a place where there is armed conflict. You don't have to do it; just decide that, whatever fear you confront by acting it out has a positive impact. Instead of climbing a mountain or running a marathon, do those things for medical research or another favorite cause. Think about the fear you wrote down and ask yourself: Is this something that is destructive? Will it hurt people? If it is, strike it out and think of something else. A good way to find a fear that is both fascinating and nontoxic is to choose something that will make a positive impact on the world. Activities that are both positive and creative—whether they be helping people in a third world country or volunteering at a hospice— can be extremely frightening. Framing your fears in this way can help you conquer them, and can result in something wonderful. Plan your progress, make your way to your goal, one step at a time, and just keep on taking that one more step on your path.

Take an Acting Class

Here are 10 ways that taking an acting course can help to succeed in your career: You learn:

1. Improvisation. (e.g., how to think and act spontaneously in different situations.)
2. Project Management.
3. How to Work with Limited resources.
4. How to Deal with Very Different Human Beings.
5. To better Understand the Human Condition.
6. How to Do Whatever Needs to Be Done.
7. About Hard work
8. How to Make Difficult Choices.
9. Presentation Skills.
10. How to Do the Best You Can With What You've Got.

Create Your Identity: Think of Yourself as a Product

1. Give yourself a title.

2. Start marketing and promoting yourself. Learn to answer the questions, "Why should I hire you? What makes you so special? What are your strengths?

3. Learn how to communicate with different audiences.

4. Have business cards, stationary, fliers, web page, etc developed to describe who you are and what you offer.

5. Talk yourself up.

6. Learn To Charge For Your Work

7. Learn The Basics of Business and Sales Techniques – Learn How to Close. Sell Something!

8. Sell Yourself! Find Out What The Going Fee For What You Are Offering.

9. $$$ Charge For Your Service!

10. Do It Once And Then Again! Get Used To Charging For Your Services!

11. Do Not Be Afraid To Ask For Money!

12. Convince Yourself That You Are Worth Your Fee!

Bibliography

---- ‑∿‑ ----

"Audre Lorde Quotes. QuotesGram." QuotesGram. Get Motivated in the Pursuit of Happiness. N.p., n.d. Web. 3 Aug. 2016.

Cook, John, ed. The Book of Positive Quotations. Minneapolis: Fairview Press, 1997. Print.

"Dream Deferred Poem by Langston Hughes - Poem Hunter." PoemHunter.com. N.p., n.d. Web. 3 Aug. 2016.

Laozi, and Archie J. Bahm. Tao the King. New York: F. Ungar Pub. Co, 1958. Print.

"Lorraine Hansberry - African-American Playwright." About.com Education. N.p., n.d. Web. 3 Aug. 2016.

"Lorraine Hansberry Biography at Black History Now." Black Heritage Commemorative Society. N.p., n.d. Web. 3 Aug. 2016.

Murphy, Trace, ed. A Book of Wisdom. New York: Image, 1995. Print.

"Neil Armstrong - 43 Quotes." Famous Quotes - Over 2.5 Million Funny, Inspirational, Life Quotes! N.p., n.d. Web. 3 Aug. 2016.

"Nelson Mandela: 11 Inspirational Quotes To Live Your Life by | World | News." The Independent. N.p., n.d. Web. 3 Aug. 2016.

Paley, Grace. Enormous Changes at the Last Minute: Stories. New York: Farrar, Straus, Giroux, 1974. Print.

Piercy, Marge. Small Changes. New York: Fawcett Columbine, 1997. Print.

"Quote by Helen Keller: "Be of Good Cheer. Do Not Think of Today's Failure..."." Goodreads. N.p., n.d. Web. 3 Aug. 2016.

"The Road Not Taken - Poetry Foundation." Discover Poetry - Poetry Foundation. N.p., n.d. Web. 3 Aug. 2016.

"ROGERS AND HAMMERSTEIN - YOU'LL NEVER WALK ALONE LYRICS."SongLyrics.com. N.p., n.d. Web. 3 Aug. 2016.

"Rosa Parks - Black History." *HISTORY.com.* N.p., n.d. Web. 3 Aug. 2016.

"The Supreme Accomplishment is to Blur the Line Between Work and Play. ... by Arnold J. Toynbee." *Positive Inspirational Quotes and Sayings.* N.p., n.d. Web. 3 Aug. 2016.

"Top Ten Neil Armstrong Quotes & Phrases." *About.com Education*. N.p., n.d. Web. 3 Aug. 2016.

Twain, Mark. ""The Two Most Important..."." N.p., Web. <www. quotesvalley.com/the-two-most-important-days-in-your-life-mark-twain/>.

Tzu, Lao, and Archie J. Brahm. *Tao Teh King: Interpreted As Nature and Intelligence*. 10th ed. New York: Frederick Ungar, 1976. Print.

Student's Guide To
Starting Your Career
AND Earning Money
BEFORE You Get Your Degree

Horace W. Batson, Ph.D.
Gary Batson, D.M.

Foreword by Dr. Leon Perkal
Associate Dean of Faculties (NYSCAS), Touro College

To Order Your Copy
EarnMoneyB4Degree.com